THE FAMILY BIBLE: A PRICELESS HEIRLOOM

Its History and Evolvement with Inscriptions of Family History Events

Rena King

THE FAMILY HISTORY PARTNERSHIP

Published by
The Family History Partnership
57 Bury New Road, Ramsbottom
Bury, Lancashire BL0 0BZ

www.thefamilyhistorypartnership.com

First published 2014

Copyright © Rena King

ISBN: 978 1 906280 39 0

**www.bibleinscriptions.co.uk
(from late 2014)**

enquiries@bibleinscriptions.co.uk

Printed and bound by
Berforts Information Press
Southfield Road, Eynsham
Oxford OX29 4JB

CONTENTS

Introduction and Acknowledgements	5
Verse: My Bible and I	7
A Short History of the Family Bible	8
Very Early Bibles	15
Verse: My Mother's Bible	22
Serendipity!	23
Earliest Recorded Entries	27
Earliest Printed Bibles and Their Owners	29
Bible Descents	32
Baptisms, Christenings, Inoculations	34
Bibles at a Price!	38
Bibles Presented by Sunday School	40
Bibles as School Prizes	42
Bibles as Births, Marriages and Gifts	44
Bibles with Congratulations	46
Bibles with Grateful Thanks	48
Enlistments and Record of Service	50
Apprenticeships and Indentures	51
Emigration	53
Deaths and Their Causes	61
Death by Drowning	63
Death by Accident	64
Deaths by Suicide and Murder	66
World War One Deaths	67
Where there's a Will.......	69
Notable Days and Weather	71
Short Verses and Poems	73
Miscellany	75
Sources	80
Surname Index	81
Place Index	85
Vessels Index	87

THE FAMILY REGISTER

Henry Brown born in Stubbekjöbing in the Island of Falster in Denmark on the 23rd of January 1835.

Caroline Brown born on the 17th Day of October 1835

Married in King Williams Town British Kafferarie on the 21st Day of June 1858

Thomas Henry Brown born in Cape Town Cape of good Hope on the 6th Day of January 1859

Brown Family Bible (ref. 0255).

INTRODUCTION AND ACKNOWLEDGEMENTS

For many years I have been collecting Bible inscriptions taken from hundreds of Bibles. It came about after I realised that too many Family Bibles, full of unique and irreplaceable inscriptions of baptisms, marriages and burials, were being thrown away or discarded. Many contained personal details unlikely to be found elsewhere. Every month in family history magazines you would read of Bibles being found at jumble sales, second hand bookshops or worse still, council rubbish tips where one was actually rescued! This kind of thing usually happened during a house clearance after the death of some elderly person with no known family.

To previous generations, the Bible was a treasured piece of family history to be passed down from generation to generation, full of intimate family information and representing an invaluable primary source of social and historic detail. In particular many inscriptions are unique as they pre-date civil registration of births, marriages and deaths. Sadly, the discovery of so many fascinating family details was in danger of being lost, so the idea of extracting all of the surnames mentioned in the Bible inscriptions and collating these into an index of surnames, was born.

However because of their bulk, I soon realised that rescuing and keeping the Bibles themselves was not an option. Basically my index was compiled from photocopies or transcripts of Bible inscriptions sent to me by family historians from an abandoned Bible or from a Family Bible they had inherited.

The spellings of surnames and places are exactly as they appear in the inscription. Sometimes an inscription can be just one or two lines, or sometimes six or more pages which is quite unusual. Judging by the letters I have received over the years, so many Family Bibles have mysteriously disappeared, perhaps to some distant unknown relation or sadly an untimely unceremonious end. Hopefully by recording the unique and irreplaceable inscriptions, the family details will live on even if the actual Bible is lost forever.

It wasn't long after I began collecting the inscriptions that I realised these were not just a list of births, marriages and deaths, but a rich and unique source of family history. They revealed a wealth of information with comments on childhood illnesses, vaccinations, apprenticeships, services, regiments, emigration dates and vessels etc., almost every subject under the sun and that included the weather too!

Who would have thought, that one day their children or grandchildren would be household names? The following famous persons are amongst the collection of Bible inscriptions.... the family events of JOHN LOUDEN MCADAM of tarmac fame; the handwritten entries for ROBERT BURNS the world famous Scottish poet and his family; transcription from a Bible - the birthday gift from CAROLINE LAMB to THE HON. WILLIAM LAMB in 1821; a transcription of many generations of the famous KEILLER family of Dundee, Confectionery Manufacturers; a photocopy of the Family Bible of ROSE FITZGERALD and her family, which lists her marriage and the birth of her children, including of course, the late President of the USA - JOHN F. KENNEDY. Genuine priceless heirlooms which thankfully have been preserved and handed down from generation to generation.

Collating all this information, creating the surname index and writing this book, has been a fascinating journey which could never have been achieved without the help of everyone who over the years sent the Bible inscriptions to me, so many thanks to everyone. However, after careful consideration my decision to include the Reference Number after each inscription is to enable correct identification of the family papers in my collection, should an enquiry be received concerning that particular surname. Finally, as well as thanking everyone else, I particularly wish to acknowledge the help and permission of Tracy St. Claire of the USA for the inclusion of some of her Bible inscriptions and helping me expand my index to other parts of the world. At the last count the total number of foreign countries mentioned in the inscriptions index amounted to sixty five, a truly worldwide coverage of Family Bibles.

Rena King

"My Bible and I"

We've travelled together
My Bible and I
Through all kinds of weather
With smile or with sigh
In sorrow or sunshine
In tempest or calm -
It's friendship unchanging
My lamp and my psalm.

We've travelled together
My Bible and I
When life had grown weary
And death e'en was nigh
But all through the darkness
Of mist or of wrong
I found there a solace
A prayer and a song.

So now who shall part us
My Bible and I?
Shall "isms" or "schisms"
Or "new lights" who try?
Shall shadow for substance
Or stone for good bread
Supplant thy sound wisdom
Give folly instead?

Ah no, my dear Bible
Exponent of light!
Thou sword of the spirit
Put error to flight!
And all thru life's journey
Until my last sigh,
We'll travel together,
My Bible and I.

Author unknown

A SHORT HISTORY OF THE FAMILY BIBLE

You can still buy large Family Bibles similar to those of a few centuries ago, with special blank pages to record all the important details of family life and death. Many family historians have been very lucky to inherit a treasured Family Bible handed down from generation to generation, full of fascinating family history and lovingly recorded for posterity in many an ancestors' handwriting. Usually the special blank pages were located between the Old and New Testaments and were richly decorated with angelic cherubs, religious scenes or brightly coloured illustrations. Many of the illustrations were of a very high quality - old masters' representations of important biblical stories and in excellent colour. In the case of smaller Bibles any blank page or flyleaf would be used to write down all the important family events. For centuries only the smaller Bibles existed and the larger Family Bibles for those that could afford them, did not appear until many years later when they were also used to hold important family papers and personal letters. Family Bibles were often huge heavy tomes measuring as much as 17inches by 11inches, 4inches thick and 10 to 12lbs in weight. The strong thick covers were usually made of leather, occasionally embossed with gold lettering with a large cross on the front. The more elaborate Bibles would have beautiful art-gilt edging with specially tooled leather binding often with brass clips to keep the Bible closed when not in use. Cassell's Illustrated Family Bible, for those unable to afford such an outright luxury, could actually be bought in separate chapters before being bound into a large book with a clasp.

In some families, the Family Bible [generally including the Book of Common Prayer] was kept in a special "Bible box" along with white gloves for the purpose of handling the cherished and sacred book. The practice of reading and seriously studying The Bible at home gradually became more widespread in the late 17th early 18th

Centuries. This was actively encouraged by the Church of England. As the head of the household, the father would have presided over the assembled family including all the servants, for evening prayers to teach and give guidance. In many of the grander homes he would sit in a great oak chair complete with panelled back and arms which was specifically kept for this purpose. Late in 1970, such a chair dating from around 1630 was bought in an antique shop for a mere £500! When smaller Bibles became easily available, everyone in the family had their own copy for private reading and at breakfast time when assembled together parents and children would read in turn. Generations later, Bible readings are still a part of everyday life in some religious families.

Family walking to church

Every Sunday was a special day, when the whole family walked to church carrying their own Bible. Very often the Church would be some distance away so occasionally they would stop to rest and read from the Bible. This would also happen on the return journey where the text of the sermon would be turned up and marked with a book mark to read at teatime during evening prayers. Bibles were often owned by poorer classes with a desire to learn and would have been a most prized and precious possession especially at a time when personal belongings were few and far between. The fact that so many Bibles have survived for generations is testimony to that. People could, and did learn a lot about various subjects from the illustrations and explanatory notes. When poor or failing eyesight or illness became a problem, the children were expected to read the Bible to their parents. Very often brothers and sisters would have to take turns at going to school because their parents could not afford the pennies to educate them all at the same time. Those same children would then have had to work in the fields during the time they were off school.

Bibles were often given as rewards and presents from parents, schools or charities and you will find many smaller Bibles given to younger children bearing the words "A gift of Lord Wharton's Trustees". According to a printed book-plate pasted inside a Bible dated 1773, the instructions, "The Reading Psalms of the Translation in the Bible, to be learned without Book by the children, are these Psalms following, viz:1, 15, 25, 37, 101, 113, 145" [Ref.0513]. To qualify for such a commendable gift, the young child was instructed to select a Biblical passage of no less than fifteen verses. This had to be thoroughly studied and understood and at least five verses had to be accurately recited. It is said that Lord Wharton's expressed intention in presenting young people with an individual Bible was to encourage their personal study and understanding of the Holy Scriptures.

Who was this charitable Lord Wharton who distributed Bibles? He was Philip, fourth Lord Wharton of Wooburn [sic] House in Buckinghamshire, who was born in 1613 and died 4th February 1696. In his Will he left 463 acres of land at Sinningthwaite in Yorkshire to a trust, to enable his work which he had started six years before his death, to continue. This work, was the purchase and distribution of Bibles and other religious books for young people to learn and understand many of his favourite Psalms. His original bequest took the form of an annual gift of ten Bibles for poor children in Wycombe and several other Buckinghamshire towns, as well as Cumberland, Westmorland and Yorkshire. To enable the people to hear the scriptures, the Bibles would be accompanied by a payment of 10 shillings to the local parson for a sermon proving the truth of the scriptures.

Lord Wharton's father, who was also a godly man, died when Philip was just nine years old and, at the still young age of thirteen, Philip went to Oxford University and subsequently travelled the continent for three years. Philip Wharton was also at one time Lord Lieutenant of the County for the Parliament during the Civil War. It is said that when the Long Parliament met, he took part in politics as a patriot. However like all the Presbyterians, Philip was against the beheading of Charles I and since he was a personal friend of Cromwell, he no longer took part in politics after the execution. Later on Philip became known as the protector of ejected Nonconformist ministers, frequently attending their secret services and known to have sheltered preachers in his own house. At the Restoration Philip welcomed Charles II, but when Parliament passed severe laws against Nonconformists, despite Charles promises made earlier, he decided to side with them. However, despite having been imprisoned in the Tower after displeasing the king, Philip lived to welcome William III to the throne and later became one of his Privy Councillors. It is said that Lord Wharton kept pictures of Van Dyck, Lely and other famous artists in his house and that it was one of the finest collections in England, unfortunately dispersed in the early 18th century. One of these paintings inscribed "Philip now Ld Wharton and Jane, Daughter and heir of Arthur Goodwin Esq, his 2d wife, and Henry their 3d sonne, about 1656" now hangs in the High Wycombe Guildhall and a superb portrait of Lord Wharton painted by Van Dyck is said to be in the Hermitage Gallery in Leningrad. Three hundred years after his death, the Trustees of Lord Wharton's Bible Charity still continue to follow his wishes and to this very day they still distribute Bibles and Prayer Books to deserving children and intend to do so throughout the foreseeable future.

12 THE FAMILY BIBLE: A PRICELESS HEIRLOOM

The Whartons of Wooburn c. 1656

ANN IMPEY HER BOOK 1773. [Bible ref.0513]

THE GIFT OF THE LATE LORD WHARTON
DISTRIBUTED BY HIS LORDSHIP'S TRUSTEES

THOMAS HIRST AGE 7. [Bible ref.0198]

THE GIFT OF LORD WHARTON'S TRUSTEES 1853.
T.W.MERCER

COLIN MCROBBIE AGED 14 YEARS [Bible ref.0299]

A GIFT FROM LORD WHARTON, RICHMOND NATIONAL
SCHOOL JANUARY 1ST 1856.

MISS MARY ANN ELIZABETH HULL 1861   [Bible ref.0003]

AS A GIFT OF PHILIP LORD WHARTON &
PRESENTED BY HIS LORDSHIP'S TRUSTEES

Sunday Schools, societies, employers, friends and family would have presented many of the smaller Bibles for a variety of reasons, whilst the larger Family Bibles, for those who could afford one, would be considered an essential item in the household. The recording of family events was an important part of life and often the Bible was the only book where information of this kind could be written. Many Bible entries record the actual time of a child's birth, as well as the date of birth and sometimes even the weight of the baby was recorded. Certainly in the mid 16th century the influence of the stars was considered most critical and a horoscope was calculated as soon as the baby was born. During Baptism the name of the officiating minister as well as the Godparents [sometimes described as Gossips or Sponsors] would be recorded as well. The practice of giving a child godparents dates back to pre-Reformation times and was confirmed in 1661 by the restoration of Anglican rites. In medieval England a certain spiritual relationship was said to exist between godparents and godchildren, which is why marriage between children and their godparents was prohibited. Normally godparents comprised two of the child's own sex and one of the other and they certainly influenced the choice of a child's Christian name.

Other interesting Bible entries were the recording of a child's illnesses, complete with dates of vaccinations and comments regarding the child's reaction to the vaccine. Many others record details of a son's enlistment into the Army, the Navy or the Clergy or give the date of emigration of sons, daughters or other family members, complete with the name of the ship and the final destination. Even the dates of apprenticeship and servitude are written down for posterity as well as numerous family addresses, most useful for locating ancestors in the census years. Unusual weather, strange events or a particularly memorable day are all written in the Bible and make truly fascinating reading. Without doubt, a Bible full of intimate family details is a priceless plethora of personal, social and historical information and it is becoming more obvious that our ancestors treasured and fervently used their Family Bible daily. Sadly many previous owners would turn in their graves if they knew the fate which had befallen their most precious but now unwanted Family Bible. For most people today, owning a Bible is taken for granted, but this was not always the case. Centuries ago just to possess one could have meant a life or death situation. To understand the reasons why, it is important to know of the historic struggles and hardships involved with the various stages of the development of the early Bibles and its eventual popularity during the past five hundred years.

> Steal not this Book my honest Friend
> For fear the gallows should be thy end,
> And when you die the Lord will say
> Where is that book you stole away?

VERY EARLY BIBLES

It is generally recognised today, that very early Bibles were brought to Britain by missionaries such as Columba and Augustine in the 6th century. These were called the Vulgate Bibles which simply meant "common" or "of the people" and for the next one thousand years these versions, written in Latin, were used by the Church throughout Europe. Prior to the Vulgate Bibles, translations of parts of the scriptures were being written by priests and monks and in the ninth century King Alfred is also said to have encouraged further translation.

Scriptorian monk

Surprisingly, it wasn't until the late 14th century that England had a whole Bible in her own language. This was the work of John Wycliffe and his loyal followers, sometimes called Lollards, who made a complete translation of the Bible from Latin into English in 1380, and as more and more people began learning to read so the demand for Bibles grew. Wycliffe and his followers had often complained that people could not understand Latin and set about this task by writing out each copy by hand. Despite this enormously laborious method, many hundreds were produced and it is thought that about 170 copies still survive today. In fact, in 1993, three early 15th century John Wycliffe handwritten Bibles were bought at Sotherby's in London for a staggering £211,200. The Wycliffe Bibles are about the size of a pocket dictionary and six hundred years ago the sight of one of these miniatures would have caused tremendous palpitations. Just to have possession of a Bible according to the then Church of Rome, was punishable by death. Following Wycliffe's handwritten miniatures, the first printed Bible in the West was produced in Germany and was known as The Gutenberg Bible. In 1454 there were around 150 copies; 120 on paper and 30 on calfskin, and of the latter only 12 have survived. Britain claims to have at least eight copies including two at the British Library. Today, a copy in impeccable condition might fetch many millions of pounds.

It was during the 15th century that many Bibles were translated and then subsequently printed into various languages throughout the Protestant countries of Europe, but it wasn't until the early 1600's that the Roman Catholic Church decided to produce their own version of the Bible. This became known as the Douay-Rheims Bible which remained their standard version until 1750, when Richard Challoner published his revision which is still widely used today.

However, it was not until 1526 when the first English language New Testament was produced. Wycliffe's earlier Bible had been voraciously banned by the Church since 1408 and sadly from this date, and with considerable efficiency, the Church had continued to track down and relentlessly destroy all the existing Wycliffe copies. Consequently, many of the English versions printed in Germany from 1454 onwards were smuggled into England hidden in bales of wool or wine casks with false bottoms by genuinely sympathetic merchants for the eager public willing to risk their lives to read them.

VERY EARLY BIBLES

Thus the Church maintained its ban on English Scriptures when a scholar of considerable reputation, William Tyndale, translated and published the New Testament from the original Greek and Hebrew into the English language. In 1524 he had left England to live on the continent and it was at Worms in 1526 where his New Testament was printed. Tyndale then began translation of the Old Testament but before he could finish, he was betrayed at Antwerp into the hands of his enemies. After sixteen months imprisonment Tyndale was tried and finally burned for heresy at the Castle of Vilvorde in October 1536 by order of the Emperor of Germany. A complete copy of Tyndale's first edition of 1526 was held by Bristol Baptist College until April 1994, when it was bought privately for one million pounds by the British Museum. The only other surviving copy, unfortunately incomplete, is held in St.Paul's Cathedral Library in London.

At the same time as Tyndale's imprisonment, Miles Coverdale a skilled writer and scholar and much favoured with the sympathy of Thomas Cromwell who was now Secretary of State, was encouraged by him to continue Tyndale's work. Cromwell had a great deal of influence with the King, Henry VIII, and this resulted in the first authorised edition of the Bible in English being printed in 1535 and known as The Great Bible. This was just months before Tyndale was burned for heresy in Europe. Cromwell was also successful in pursuing these sympathies and succeeded in having a licence granted. Consequently, Tyndale translations began to reappear despite previous banning of all Bibles under his name.

In 1537 another version appeared and this Bible had been translated by a "Thomas Matthew", thought to be a friend of Tyndale. Later however, Cromwell commissioned Coverdale again to produce a revision of this work and this was known as Cranmer's or The Great Bible. This appeared in 1539 and was sold for 13s.4d "unless Cromwell would give the printers exclusive privileges, when they might be sold for 10s". This later version was much favoured by Henry VIII who then commanded that every Church should possess one. However these Bibles were so expensive that parish councils often used a chain to fasten the Bible to the lectern for fear of them being stolen. Great crowds of the common people flocked to church to hear the new and wonderful words from the Bible spoken for the first time in their mother tongue. The joy was overwhelming, as the ability to read was looked upon as the most enviable of human acquirements.

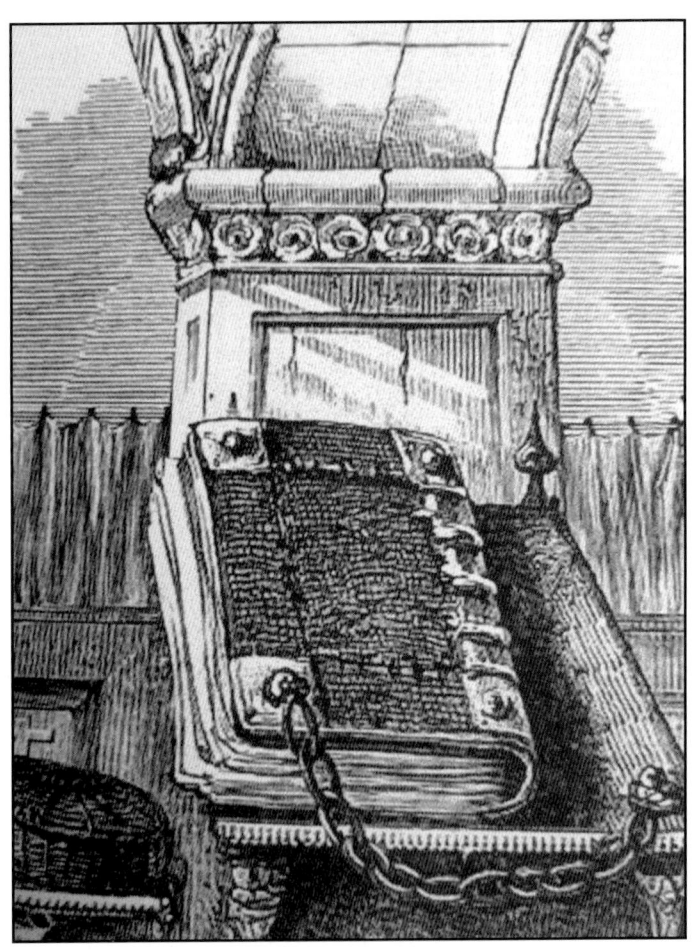

Bible chained to lectern

During the reign of Bloody Mary [1553-1558], Protestants were again persecuted as heretics and many fled to the European countries as refugees. Geneva was a strong Protestant city and it was here in 1560 that a group of refugees including one William

Whittingham, produced, published and printed a complete revision of the Bible using for the first time Roman type with verse divisions. This was known as the Genevan "Breeches Bible" because of the substitution of the word "breeches" for "aprons" in Gen. 3:7 referring to Adam and Eve covering themselves up with fig leaves. It was to become the most popular English Bible for over half a century. By 1568, during the reign of Elizabeth I, another revision had appeared known as the Bishop's Bible, but at that time it never saw the popularity of the Geneva Bible.

However it was not until 1604 when yet another revision of the Bible was proposed, welcomed and sponsored by the new King, James I. This was done on a grand scale with around fifty translators appointed to work in six groups each being responsible for a section of the text from the now favoured Bishop's Bible. Eventually this revision was completed in 1611 and became known as the King James Version or the Authorised Version surpassing many earlier translations in authority and power. It is generally thought that no book had greater influence on the English language and today it remains the most important and much loved Bible of all times.

Apart from many minor Bible translations, it was to be some 250 years after the Reformation in the 16th century, before anyone attempted a new major revision of the Bible. The decision to revise the 1611 King James Version arose due to the discovery of many old manuscripts, particularly the New Testament manuscripts, which were found to be much older than those on which the Authorised Version of the Bible was based. This was agreed at the Convocation of Canterbury in 1870 and in 1881 the New Testament of the Revised Bible was published, followed by the complete Bible in 1885.

It was not until 1988, when the 400th anniversary of the Welsh Bible was celebrated, that the first full translation of the Bible from English into Welsh was produced. This was achieved by Bishop William Morgan of Ty Mawr Wybrnant, Caernarvonshire together with a group of North Wales scholars. Many felt it restored the respect and dignity of the Welsh language which had almost disappeared and was looked upon as one of the most significant events in the religious and cultural history of Wales and Welsh speaking people. The Bible served not only as a religious text but also as a grammar textbook and reading aid. This was particularly true for school children as often it was the only book available. Around 1786 this was especially true in the case of Sunday Schools which were set up throughout Wales under the inspiration of one Rev.Thomas Charles who made sure they were well supplied with Bibles. Such was the importance of owning a copy of the Welsh Bible that, in 1800, Mary Jones aged sixteen from Llanfihangel-y-Pennant,in Merioneth, walked almost 30 miles from her home to Bala, to buy a copy of a new edition from the Rev.Thomas Charles. On reaching the minister's home Mary was heartbroken to be told he had no more Bibles for sale. In order to afford a copy Mary had learned to read and saved for six years the sum of three shillings and six pence so that she could buy her own Bible. The Rev. Thomas Charles was so moved by the self-sacrifice of this young girl that he managed to find her a Bible and later used his influence to help found the British and Foreign Bible Society in 1804. By 1854, just five decades later, the society had circulated 28 million Scriptures in 152 languages and dialects. In 2004 the British & Foreign Bible Society celebrated its Bicentenary at St. Paul's Cathedral in London, addressed by the Archbishop of Canterbury with over two thousand guests from Bible Societies attending from all over the world.

    Since the start of the 20th century, many new versions and translations have been produced putting the Bible into, "simple straight forward English". The most successful of these and rapidly becoming a best seller, was a New Testament in "Today's English Version" called "Good News for Modern Man" and was the very first incarnation of what became the "Good News Bible". This was produced by the Bible Society and Collins, set by computer and printed on one of the most up to date printing presses in Britain with distribution in it's first year reaching eight million copies. Within ten years, the unprecedented worldwide circulation record of sixty million copies was achieved, as well as being translated into over two thousand different languages. Today it is Britain's top selling Bible and continues to be sent to all corners of the world.

In economic terms the majority of old Bibles, even in good condition, are unlikely to have any large cash value and invariably end up being shipped abroad to America or the poorer countries by numerous Bible charities. These can be found for sale on internet websites, often on a daily basis. Several of today's Booksellers, particularly those specialising in selling old Bibles, will not consider buying anything printed after 1600! The Bibles that do sell for huge sums of money today are the rarest and oldest examples in extremely good condition. Historically speaking - to a family historian - most old Family Bibles are priceless and will without doubt continue to form part of our unique written heritage for many years to come, the following pages are testimony to that.

Cherubs carrying Bibles

"My Mother's Bible"

This book is all that's left me now
Tears will unbidden start,
With faltering lips and throbbing brow
I press it to my heart.
For many generations passed
Here is our family tree;
My mother's hands this Bible clasped
She dying, gave it me.

Ah well do I remember those
Whose names those records bear,
Who round the hearthstone used to close
After the ev'ning prayer,
And speak of what this volume said
In tones my heart would thrill
Though they are with the silent dead
Here are they living still.

My Father read this Holy book
To brothers, sisters dear,
How calm was my poor Mother's look
Who loved God's word to hear.
Her angel face, I see it yet
What thronging memories come,
Again that little group is met
Within the halls of home.

Thou truest friend, man ever knew
Thy constancy I've tried,
When all were false, I found thee true
My counsellor, my guide.
The mines of earth no treasures give
From me this book could buy,
For teaching me the way to live,
It taught me how to die.

By Mary Ann Bowyer (1818-1886) (ref. 0230)

SERENDIPITY!

Many strange things are written in Family Bibles but it is difficult to believe that the owner of this Bible actually read and counted every word, or did he? "This Bible contains 3,386,489 letters; 173,692 words; 31,173 verses; 1,189 Chapters; 66 books. Fred Paine, Penshurst Station". What kind of Bible it was, we do not know, but we do know it was given to him by his sister Caroline on April 3rd,1889 when he was just 14 years old. Apart from biblical verses there are no other words written on the flyleaf (ref.0264).

Following a list of six children born during the years 1829-1836 to William Haughton & his wife Ellen Ferguson, are the words...... "The above children, not being baptised nor their names registered in the books of the Unitarian congregation of Strand Street, Dublin of which I am a member, I hereby certify that the above registry is correct, the name of each child inserted very shortly after its birth. Their beloved mother died on the 13th September 1838 having given birth to a male baby in that day who only lived for one day. Wm. Haughton". Written alongside each child is the exact time of birth they were born as well as their actual weight at birth. Following on, another page is taken up with a loving and glowing appreciation of his wife after her unfortunate death in childbirth (ref.1383).

Another Family Bible belonging to Ellen [Haughton] - the youngest daughter of the unfortunate mother who died in childbirth in the previous Bible inscription - records the horrifying shipwreck of "Ellen Haughton, her husband [Dr. Robert Lynn Heard] her eldest and only child at that time [aged 10 months old] and her father in law, survived the wreck of the CERES off Carnsore Point [Co. Wexford, Ireland] 10 November 1866. She was the only woman saved" [9 crew and 29 passengers drowned]. (ref.1384). The Bible also diligently records the exact time and weights of the children even going as far as stating "not weighed, too small" and others weighed at birth 8 ½ pounds + flannel petticoat" and "weighed 8 ½ pounds + 1½ in copper"? How intriguing the last entry is. (ref.1384).

Weighing baby

The Brown Family Bible has the following unusual entry......."31st May 1900 Thomas Brown accidentally lost his left eye at Messrs. Wm. Fox & Sons" (ref.0351).

Welsh Family Bibles were often printed and entries written in the Welsh language "Rhodd Mr. James Morris, Blaenmergi Bridell, H Charit Evans, Tynewyd Rhagfyr 26 1862 Yr hon a anuyd 30 ofis medi yn y flwydyn 1803" (ref.0346).

SERENDIPITY

The household Bible of Robert Burns the world famous Scottish poet is inscribed with the words ..."Maxwell born 26th July 1796 the day of his Father's Funeral, so named after Dr. Maxwell the Physician who attended the Poet in his last illness. Inserted by W.N. Burns [son] 9th April 1867" (ref.1414). The original Bible is preserved at Burns Cottage Museum, Alloway, Ayr, Scotland.

Written on the flyleaf inside a Bible were the following words . . . "This Bible was seized for the Education Rate (so-called)(sic) at Wheathampstead; sold at Harpenden Police Station 20th Nov.1903; purchased by the Harpenden Free Church Council and returned to the owner, Mrs.Pearson. Signed, on behalf of Harpenden F.C.C. Francis Woodmass, Sec." (ref.0260). Unfortunately they do not state how much it was sold for or why it was taken!

Most surprising to find recorded in a Family Bible was a household census. Whether or not it was prompted by the national 1801 census (just noting population numbers not names), will probably never be known . . . "March 1801 James (CHARLES) head of household of three males and two females" (ref.0500).

Written on a front end-paper of this Bible, is an amazing piece of family history . . . "We came to Llanfairfechan to live Aug.20, 1884 at Penmaen Villa. 1889 Oct.21: Commenced the work of building Hafod y Coed, Llanfechan by cutting down trees. Nov.19: Foundation commenced. 1890 July 17: we slept for the first time at Hafod y Coed." Bible of the Davies family (ref.2273).

In a similar vein the following was recorded inside the Holtham Family Bible . . . "The First Night that me and my family slept at the New house was the sixth of April 1795. [signed] Harper Holtham" (ref.2268).

A very useful piece of information such as the following was found in a Family Bible . . . "Surname changed by Deed Poll 17th July 1918" from Wollstein to Wollaston (ref.0533).

Whilst the above was probably a consequence of the First World War, so were the following events in this family ...."The Great War 1914-1915 [sic] War declared by England Aug. 4 1914. Herbert John Chappell mobilised Aug. 1914. Herbert John Chappell sailed for France Nov 4 1914 (accompanied by Bryan & Russell Latham,

26   THE FAMILY BIBLE: A PRICELESS HEIRLOOM

his cousins) also . . . Charles Gresham Chappell joined up as a Cadet & received his commission as 2nd Lt. RA" (ref.0854).

It must have been a very special baptism on the day, "Florence Mary Osmond born January 25th 1869, 3am Monday baptised by the Rev. A.A. Isaacs Aug.26th 1869 in water from the river Jordan" (ref.2276).

```
ANNA DAVIES is my name
And Welse is my nation,
LLANSLPHAN is my dwelling plase
And Christ is my salvation,
When i am dead and in my graeve
And all my boons (sic) are rhottn
In this book you will find my name
When I am quite forgottn
```

June the 8th 1864 (ref.0137)

EARLIEST RECORDED ENTRIES

Some of the inscriptions are remarkably old in comparison to the forementioned entries and certainly relate to events which took place many centuries ago. Here is a selection using the exact spellings as written in the Bibles.

[Tho]mas Rigden was baptized the 29th of July 1581 in the [pa]rish of [?] Hardres and borne in Petham (ref.2281).

M. Allandson 1585 (ref.0359).

George Harvey. Joshua the Son of George and Elizabeth Harvey was born August 19th.1588 (ref.0352).

Thomas Cartmell 1612-1682 (ref.0449).

Margret Stonestrete was born 21 November 1630 (ref.0321).

March the first day 1654 Ann Hunt dau. of Robert Hunt was born baptised as appeareth by the Registrar Mr.L.Bambridge (ref.0567).

29 July 1663 birth of John Binns at Clough Heigh (ref.1236).

June 12: Sara Fulliloue was born 1668 March 2: Mary Fulliloue was born 1669 be twixt twellf and one in the daye. (ref.0123).

Thomas Hunt - His Book - God give him grate - on it to look. Written Aprill the 23, 1682 (ref.0246).

John Poynor son of Thomas 27 Dec.1691 being St. John's Day alf an hower after 12 of ye clok and baptized 15th Jan 1692 (ref.0002).

Jonathan Warren born Dec. 8 - 1694 died Mch 11 - 1767 Esther his wife born Sep.15 - 1693 died Mch.4 - 1774 (ref.0060).

John Madox born in Kinsale on Septembr 18th 1697 and on the -- Decembr 1722 married Ann Fowle the dafther of Mr. Sam.Fowle wine cooper living in Broad St, Bristol (ref.0016).

Old Bibles

EARLIEST PRINTED BIBLES AND THEIR OWNERS

Occasionally a flyleaf would show when and where the Bible was printed and also the names of the people who were actually able to purchase a Bible all those centuries ago.

PRINTED 1578   FRANCIS BIBLE (ref.0585)

"The Newe Testament. Imprinted at London by Christopher Barker printer to the Queenes Majestie 1578".
Entries from 1697.

PRINTED 1582   ALLANDSON/ALLANSON BIBLE (ref.0359)

"Imprinted in London by Christopher Barker 1582".
Entries dating from 1585.

PRINTED 1599   JNO.HARDING (ref.0564)

Bible printed 1599. No further entries.

PRINTED 1599   FULLILOVE BIBLE (ref.0123)

"Imprinted at London by the Deputies of Christopher Barker, printer to the Queenes most excellent Majestie".
Entries from 1668.

PRINTED 1602   DAVID BIBLE (ref.0582)

> "Imprinted at London by Robert Barker, printer to the Queene". Earliest entry 1737.

PRINTED 1608   THOMAS/DAVIES/COVE BIBLE (ref.0562)

> "Imprinted at London by Robert Barker 1608".
> Entries dating from 1757.

PRINTED 1608   PETER HIGSON/JONES BIBLE (ref.0311)

> Bible printed by Robert Barker, London.
> Earliest date 1660.

PRINTED 1612   CARTMEL BIBLE (ref.0449)

> Book is second edition of Authorised Version printed in London by Robert Barker, printer to the King.
> Entries from 1612.

PRINTED 1614   NICKOLS BIBLE/BOOK OF COMMON PRAYER (ref.0466)

> Entries dating from 1717.

PRINTED 1619   HUNT BIBLE (ref.0246)

> "Imprinted at London by Bonham Norton and John Bill, printers to the Kings most excellent Majestie MDCXIX".
> Entries dating from 1682.

PRINTED 1622   STONESTRETE BIBLE (ref.0321)

    Entries dating from 1630.

PRINTED 1625   FAIRMAN BIBLE (ref.0354)

    James VI 1625. Translated from original Greek. Entries dating from 1712.

PRINTED 1634   ADAMS BIBLE (ref.0002)

    Entries dating from 1691.

Early printing establishment

BIBLE DESCENTS

> Francis Wynn Her Book March ye 15th 1757
> This Book my child to you I give
> See that 'tis never sold;
> But let it go from Heir to Heir,
> As I to you have told.....(ref.0277)

Many an ancestor assumed the treasured Family Bible would be passed down from generation to generation hoping that the recording of family events would continued long after their death. To this end many wrote in the Bible hoping that their wishes would be carried out as requested in the verse above.

"This Bible was my great grandfather's John Ffloyd, Citizen of London and comb maker by trade he lived in one of his own houses on the north side of Ludgate Hill in the parish of St.Brides and having gave his Son and Daughter a fortune and being in good circumstances he left off Trade and Retired to Wandsworth in the County of Surrey where he dyed. And it is my desire when it shall please God to take me out of this world that this Bible may be the property of my Son Ffloyd and I request him to preserve, and at his death to give it to his Son if he has one, with an injunction for him to keep it and dispose of it at his Death if he has a Son, in the same manner and so to go from Father to Son. This is my earnest request. In witness whereof I have this fifth day of December 1754 Subscribed my name to it. George Peck." (ref.0963).

"This book did belong to Mrs. Judith Simpson (died 1809) afterwards to her sister Mrs Elizabeth Bloss (died 1812) By her desire it was presented to their nephew Lawrence Watson Wood" (ref.0268).

"I, Arthur Beverley, am the owner of this book and at my death [it] shall be handed over to my younger brother Alfred Beverley. Signed March 1st,1910 Arthur Beverley." (ref.0099). His wishes were obviously carried out because on another page was written - "In the event of my death, this Bible must be handed over to my brother Tom. Signed Alfred Beverley August 10th, 1919".

"Samuel & Eliza White White (sic) who were married in Adelaide, S.A. June 16,1853, leave this Bible to their children. It belonged to their grandfather S.W.W. of Farncombe". Happily this Bible is still in the possession of direct descendant Peter Francis White (ref.1211).

Meeting new baby

BAPTISMS, CHRISTENINGS, INOCULATIONS

One of the early baptisms for the Wheler family concerns "Sophia Wheler born at Bath, in the parish of Walcot April 17: 1777 Sophe Wheler inoculated for the Small Pox at Bath, Sept. 1779 vz. had it very favourably only some spots upon her". In the same Family Bible there is an entry for Jane Wheler, daughter of the 7th Baronet, who married George Dandridge at Henley upon Thames Sept.5th 1795. "Had Issue. Lucy born on board the Melville Castle Indiaman at sea 7th December 1796. Inoculated for the Small Pox at Tipperah 22nd Feby.1799 and had it very favourably. Had the Hooping Cough at Calcutta the year following & the Scarlet fever in England the next year. Had the Chicken Pox at Bath 1804. She married on 15th October 1817 Sir Trevor Wheler 9th Baronet" (ref.0959).

For centuries, particularly in Europe and Asia, inoculation of some kind or other had been practised. However it wasn't until the 18th century that vaccination in England began with the work of Edward Jenner. Vaccination Acts followed in 1840, 1867, 1871, 1873 and in 1885 when the Royal Commission recommended the abolition of penalties against those not conforming, with further Acts 1898 and 1907. Apparently, Vaccination Certificates were given to the family and the following are transcripts of certificates found within the pages of the Family Bible.

"Vaccination Act.
Hugh Thomas Harwood child of George Harwood age 3 months born at 7 Jackson Row, M/C [Manchester] dated 9 Aug.1869"

"Compulsory Vaccination Act.
Margaret Harwood age 3 months child of George Harwood of 7 Jackson Row [1867]"

> "Compulsory Vaccination Act.
> Hannah Harwood age 3 months child of
> George Harwood [of] No. 24 Cumberland
> dated 6 June 1865" (ref.1393).

Most Family Bibles list the children's names and dates of baptism, but Edward and Sophia Kensington recorded unique information unlikely to be found elsewhere [apart from the church baptism entry].

> "Hannah Sophia Kensington born Feby. 14th 1814
> in New Bridge St, Black Friars.
>
> Baptised by the Rev. S. Good, March 5, 1814.
> Vaccinated twice in April 1814.
>
> Christened by my brother the Revd. Chas. Brown in
> New Bridge Street, Feby. 7th, 1815
>
> Sponsors: Mrs Monier Williams, Dear Sister in law,
> Mrs B Brown and Dear Brother George.
>
> Vaccinated for the third time the 20th March 1815.
> Had the Chicken Pox at home, 21st Feby. 1818.
>
> Had the Measles at Home, 1st April 1824."

[There is no explanation as to why she was Baptised so soon after birth and then Christened a year later or why she was vaccinated three times. Edward and Sophia had numerous children baptised and vaccinated from 1807 to 1814 (ref.0098).

Inoculation entries appear regularly in the Family Bible for the Hiron family and although not the first born, John Franklin Hiron christened 22nd October 1804, "was inoculated for the Cowpox and had the Hooping Cough in the year 1805. He had the Measles in November 1807" (ref.0985).

All the important details regarding the children of John Yarde Fownes and Margaret his wife were entered into the Family Bible beginning with their daughter Maria Somerville Fownes and how she was "inoculated for and passed the Cowpox December 1800 and passed the Chickenpox May1802, passed the Scarlet Fever October 1804, the measles March 1805, the Hooping Cough 1811." (ref.2239).

Around the same time "John Wilson [born July 20th,1809] was inoculated for the cow pox and went through the desease in all its stages and was two years after inoculated for small pox and had only an inflamed arm which rose but the constitution was not in the least affected." (ref.1739).

No recorded date when vaccination took place but it was written in the Family Bible, "H.C. Collamore has been vaccinated, has had the measles and the Hooping Cough. Eliza Collamore has been vaccinated. Helen Collamore has been vaccinated. May 1846 Catherine H., Eliza & Helen Collamore have had the Measles." (ref.1801).

Large baptismal font

The family of William Francis Kingwell and Mary Elizabeth his wife of Exeter consisted of eleven children whose births and occasional early deaths were dutifully entered into the Family Bible, but written alongside Cedric Dudley Kingwell born on 8th July 1888 was the blunt statement, "not registered to avoid Vaccination". (ref.0044).

An apparently sickly child seems to have been the unfortunate "Charles Frederick Nash born 6 April 1860 bt. (?baptised) Hawkhurst, Kent. Measles Oct. 1860; Mumps July 1861; Gastric fever Feb.1862; Hooping cough Mar. 1862; Chicken pock Mar. 1863; Small pox Mar. 1867; St.Vitus Feb. 1869; Died 23 Jan. 1882 buried Elstree Church. Exhaustion after fits"! (ref.0353).

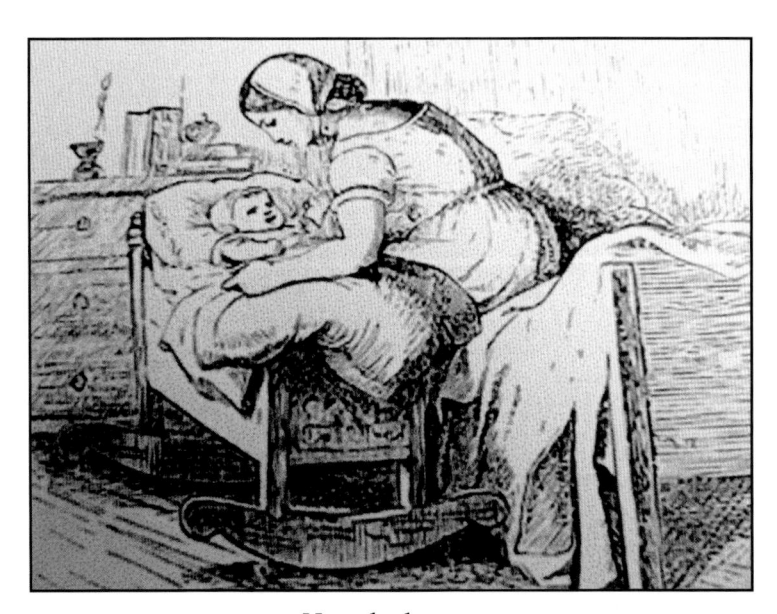

New baby

BIBLES AT A PRICE!

As well as Bibles being passed down through successive generations, there were numerous charities distributing free Bibles. Many people would have made many sacrifices just to own one.

Found written inside a very old Bible: "John Hatson his book Costt 2s bought att Northswitch the 4th day oft March 1676" (ref.0568).

Perhaps the following was the kind of Bible bought in instalments? Written on the flyleaf of the Family Bible of Samuel and Tryphena Baldwin was- "The Gift of my Mother Hester, pd. for binding 15s" dated c.1724 (ref.0407).

Slightly more expensive perhaps; a Bible bought by "John & Anne Gibben. Their book bought in Chesterfield the 30th day of Octr.1754 price one pound" (ref.0314).

Another interesting anecdote, presumably written by the then present owner of the Bible Rev. Francis L. Denman dated Jan.19, 1906 - "Old Spanish Bible from the late Lord Hatherley's sale 1887 which fetched £3-17-6" (ref.0619).

Interestingly, the words "Isaac Worthington/Robert Johnson's Booke 1762" are written on a Bible's title page with the following printed wording "London. Printed by Edw. Jones for Abel Small at the "Unicorn" and Henry Bonwicke at the "Red Lion" in St. Paul's Churchyard. MDCLXXXIX" and followed by the fascinating title "The General History/ of the / Reformation /of the / Church/ from the errors & corruptions of the/ Church of Rome/ Begun in Germany/ by Martin Luther/ with the progress thereof in all parts of Christendom/ from the Year 1517 to the Year 1556. Written in Latin/ by John Sleidan LLD/ and faithfully established/ to which is added/ a continuation/ to the end of the council of Trent in the

BIBLES AT A PRICE! 39

Year 1562/ by Edmund Bohun Esq." There then follows a handwritten historical account of the life and times of John Sleidan written by Hessel Levinsohn, Missionary of the British Society among the Jews (ref.0598).

Old book with magnifyer

BIBLES PRESENTED BY SUNDAY SCHOOLS

Apart from Lord Wharton's Charity, the presentation and giving of Bibles was by various associations and individuals. Bibles were given for a great variety of reasons such as a birthday, Christmas or a wedding gift. Many were given for long service or in the case of Sunday Schools for exemplary attendance, abilities and good behaviour. Sunday School Bibles tended to be of the smaller variety not larger Family Bibles and generally they were not used to record details of other family members but this was not always the case.

Many Bible presentations would have been similar to the following, so perhaps it is heartening to learn that this Bible is still with Joseph's descendants, "This Bible was presented by the Committee and Teachers of Lombard Street, Sabbath School, to Joseph Westbury as an honourable testimony of their regard on his dismission from the School / October 20th, 1822". (ref.1081).

A Book of Common Prayer was "Given as a reward for good behaviour and progress in learning, by the Conductors of Swineshead Sunday School to James Wilson. Dec.1st A.D.1836". There follows a list of Butler births from 1868 to 1883 on a flyleaf but it is not clear whether they are related to James Wilson or not (ref.0280).

A Holy Bible was given to "Edward Williams the gift of Swan Hill Sabbeth School September 8th 1839. JW" for what reason remains unknown (ref.1505).

From a Bible "Presented to Jane Swingler on her leaving Harborough Independent Sabbeth School June 21st 1846 in Kind Rememberance" (ref.0388).

"Given by the Friends of Milton Sunday School to Mary Hurst November 1853" (ref.1318).

Similarly "A Reward to John William Watson from the Wesleyan Sunday School Kirkby Bain for early attendance and good behaviour August 23,1874. R.M." This Bible seems to have been

BIBLES PRESENTED BY SUNDAY SCHOOLS 41

passed down a few generations and used as a family register as the last entry is dated 1942." (ref.0288).

It is not clear if this recipient was a pupil or a teacher. "John Matthews. This Bible was presented to John Matthews by the Rev.Thomas John Martin(?)leaving the Sunday School, Gittisham" (ref.1227).

Written inside another Bible "Presented to Christina Drover as a small token of respect for her valuable and disinterested [sic] services in teaching the young for a number of years in Junction Street Sabbath Evening School, North Leith. Dec.16th 1851" (ref.0400).

The following inscription appears inside the front cover of a Bible "Presented to Miss Wanstall, by the members of the Norton Church Choir, as a small token of regard. March 1868" (ref.0113).

On the first page of the Family Bible of Alice and Edward James Dibben is written "From the Poole Ladies Bible Association 1840." (ref.0482).

"Presented to Frederick Skinner by the Officers and Teachers of the Wesleyan Sunday School, Irchester June 30th '89. With Best Wishes for his future welfare. Stephen Parsons, Superintendent" (ref.0628).

Most unusual was the following inscription written in a Bible "Presented to The Rev. Wm. Allen 3rd at his recognition into the Wesleyan Ministry. Leeds Conference 1845. Jacob Stanley President, Rt. Newton Secretary" and followed by the words "Ordained Nov.10,1841 in the Mission House before I went abroad. W.A." (ref.0221).

A decorative bookplate headed "The Salvation Army Young People's War East Ham Corps. Presented to ARTHUR BUTLER for Good Conduct, Diligence and Regular Attendance obtained Finale Marks out of a possible __ "Be thou an Example". Signed: P.M. Hutton, C.O, W.J.Foskett Sergt. Major, Date: Jan.1937" (ref.0067).

A large Prayer Book - published 1754 simply states "Fellowship of Pilots, Deal. Presented to Mr. Thomas Neyland July 27th 1851. J.W.Arnold" (ref.1480) - with no explanation as to why it was given as a present.

BIBLES AS SCHOOL PRIZES

Bibles presented by Schools as prizes were also very popular just as they are today . . . "St.George's Church Secondary School, Reading. Prize to ALBERT GROVE for Attendance, Lessons, Conduct. Christmas 1890. John Stewart, vicar" (ref.0279).

Similarly, "Children going to school.Children going to school.This book from the Salop Archidiaconal Board of Education was given by the Wellington Chapter as the first prize to JOHN WOLLSTEIN of Upton Magna School 30 July 1859. Geo.L.Yate, Rural Dean" (ref.0533).

It was not just the pupils who received Bibles.

Teacher and children

A letter of affection accompanied the Bible presented to this teacher. "Sept.18,1865. Dear Teacher, We hope you will receive the Sacred present as a token of our love from 6 of your scholars.Emma Robinson; Elizabeth Smith; Clara Green; Harriet Fox; Ellen Suffolk; Elizabeth West. We wish You many happy returns of the day." (ref.2274). Unfortunately the teacher's name was not mentioned but she may have been Florence GRIFFIN who passed the Bible on to her descendants.

Finally, "To Mr.Charles MILLARD on his retirement from the Office of Master to the Woburn British Free School in acknowledgement of his strict attention and endeviating attention to duty during a period of 30 years. With sincere respect for high character and a friendly regard to his future interests, this Bible is presented by the committee and subscribers. Dec. 23rd 1853. H.Veasey, Secretary" (ref.0131).

Children going to school

BIBLES AS BIRTHS, MARRIAGES AND GIFTS

Bibles as marriage gifts were numerous and not just by one friend to another as recorded on a bookplate inside the Bible of "Mr. Harry Boxall by the members of the New Barnet Baptist Men's Bible Class on the occasion of his marriage to Miss Annie Dolton September 4th 1913" (ref. 1501).

"To William and Eliza Cousens July 13, 1878 being the first couple married in the New Church at Twyford. By R.Buston, vicar." (ref.1510).

"Presented to John and Martha Llewellyn on the Occasion of their Marriage by Samuel and Amelia Willing in commemoration of theirs being the first Wedding in the Chapel; and as an expression of esteem and Christian Love. Deuteronomy 11 Chapter.18-21 Verses. Mount Pleasant Baptist Chapel, Pembroke August 29th 1865" (ref.1506).

A Bible published in 1884 bears the following "Presented to Miss Jane Quarrington on the eve of her marriage by her fellow teachers in the Dale Grove Sunday School - North Finchley August 1890 Psalm CXX1 verses 5-8" (ref.0024).

Most beautifully inscribed is the following inscription "The Organist and a Few Friends at York Place, Oxford Road, Congratulate MISS BEBB upon her approaching Marriage, and with the best wishes For Her Future Happiness and Prosperity, beg her to accept this Bible as a slight token of their esteem and regard. Manchester September 14th, 1872" (ref.0316).

"Jno. Davis & Mary Brown wase married the 2nd of May 1803, by the Revn'd Newport, clergyman In the parish of Claines in Worcestershire, after 5 years of cortship wile servant to Miss Browings in the Tything, wich wase a Good mistress & a Charatable Christins" (ref.0016).

On a more personal note "To William and Mary Ann Noble on the occasion of their marriage from Rev. A.H.and Mrs.Gay. Oct. 14th 1882" (ref.0355).

"To Emma Sanders on her marriage with prayers for her future happiness from Harry Corles her loving Uncle, Langham St. Mary Rectory, Suffolk January 1868" (ref.1326).

Newspaper cuttings are often enclosed within the pages of Family Bibles but in this instance an actual birth certificate about five inches by three inches was stuck inside the Family Bible of the Hadfield family showing Sophia Hadfield (nee Howarth) was born on 15 Oct.1843. Interestingly, she was several weeks under sixteen years of age when she married on 4 September 1859 and gave birth to eleven children from 1861 to 1886 (ref.0026).

Another young bride "Married in July 20, 1879 in Berkley Church, Gloucestershire Sarah Ann Spragg age 16 years (to) William Coalman age 21 years" (ref.1609).

Many inscriptions are just a line or two "Cecilia Margaret Whitting from her Godfather John Gregory Forbes March 14,1871" (ref.0550).

"Eileen Ann Parker from her God Mother C.Kerr July 30th 1939 The Day of her Baptism" (ref.1518).

"Frances Smith Smith (sic) - from Mrs.Hardy in Rememberance of her Confirmation Nov.22nd and Final Communion Christmas Day 1914. Chilham" (ref.0417).

"This Bible presented to Henry Albert Kaull on Attaining his 5th Birthday by his Grandma Soper. 25th day of Oct,1879" (ref.0096).

Needless to say many Bibles were presented on every conceivable birthday from the first right through to a 35th Birthday........ "James John Barker, Bletchley - December 26th, 1882 For A New Years Gift. Was 16 years and 4 months old when I had this Holy Bible" (ref.0396).

"William Howley Goodenough from his Godfather W. Cantuary, Lambeth March 16,1837." William was actually born in 1833 son of "Edmund Goodenough, Dean of Wells & Frances his wife" and married 1st Sept. 1874 in Vienna, Countess Anna Kinsky born Aug. 23,1852 daughter of Count Eugene Kinsky (of) Austria" (ref.0621).

BIBLES WITH CONGRATULATIONS

Occasionally there is mention of happier events written alongside family details.

Was it Mrs. Chas Gram who wrote in her book that "Mrs.Wesson of Helpston reached her 100th birthday on June 30th 1923, not only were church bells rung but she rec'd a telegram from King & Queen" (ref.0358).

I wonder if "Margaret Davidson died Dec, 14th 1817 aged 102" received a telegram too? (ref.0005).

Congratulations were recorded as "John & Priscilla Christianna Bedingfield, celebrate their Silver Wedding, Dec. 25th 1906" (ref. 0025).

Village church

Taken from the Family Bible of John Henry Croucher born in London on 7th December 1851. Apparently he emigrated to Australia in 1879, where he married Mary McArthur a New Zealander. Today the Bible remains in the possession of his Australian descendants with a [newspaper?] cutting congratulating - "GOLDEN WEDDING. Sun (Melbourne) CROUCHER-ANDERTON. Mr & Mrs A.E. Croucher announce with pleasure the 50th Anniversary of their marriage, celebrated at Dorcas Street Presbyterian Church, South Melbourne June 11,1910" (ref.0023).

Even Royalty were not ignored, written inside this Bible "Elizabeth Mortimer of Harrogate Sunday School Union. Queen Victoria Diamond Jubilee 22.6.1897" (ref.0438).

Something slightly different - a complete transcript of the 1826 marriage of William Carver and Catherine Way was copied by the rector into the Family Bible. He also wrote "The above was extracted verbatim from the parish register of marriages in SHORWELL Parish by me Walter St. John Milding, Rector of Shorwell May 14, 1828" (ref.0998).

BIBLES WITH GRATEFUL THANKS

Employers sometimes handed out Bibles to loyal servants.

"Presented to Michael Knight with the best wishes of E. Mathews after the long servitude of twenty one years with her father. November 1861" (ref.0140).

However by contrast, "This Bible is presented to Betty Robinson by the Manchester Society for the Improvement and Encouragement of Female Servants, as a Reward for her satisfactory Services in the employ of Miss Hall of Ordsall Hill. Sept. 23rd 1829" (ref.0309).

Another employer wrote inside this Bible "To Rebecca Gay a testimony of regard for faithful services in the family of Samuel Sampson. 20th March 1860" (ref.1610).

"This Bible was given to John Ashford by his Master H.G. Kerstemeem? in rememberence of his faithful and good conduct during the period of five years & upwards he lived with him. Exeter Jan.y. 28th 1837" (ref.0510).

Many inscriptions leave the reader in no doubt as to why a Bible was given, but not as in this case "Victoria Mary Newton (gave) to her dear Nurse Mary Ann Geldart July 4th 1866" a copy of the Holy Bible (ref.0068).

In a similar vein . . . "To Francis Thomas Van Hemert Esq. This Sacred Book is presented as a momento of the late Mrs. Seddon with the grateful regards of her husband and children, for his kind and valuable services during a lengthened illness from which she was released and thro' the Grace of her Saviour Borne to Her Everlasting "Home" June 21st 1861. Christ Church Parsonage St. Kilda" (ref.0489). Was he her doctor?

An emotional time perhaps, when a Bible bearing the arms and the words of St. Bartholomew's Hospital 1858 on the outer cover, was presented as . . . "This Bible and the accompanying Prayer Book were used by Mrs. Mary Ann Evans on the occasion of her attending Devine Service in the Church of St. Bartholomew the

Less for the last time in her official capacity as Sister of Hope's Ward in St. Bartholomew's Hospital, the duties of which station she so faithfully and efficiently performed for the long period of 40 years as justly to entitle her to the respect and esteem of the Governors of this Hospital in whose names these books are presented to Mrs. Evans by William Foster White, Treasurer. 22nd July 1860" (St. Bartholomew's records confirmed Mrs. Evans as being of 71 years of age and that she was granted her full pay of one guinea per week for life to be paid quarterly) (ref.0155).

It must have been a very special occasion, when a Bible embossed with a crown and feathers on the front cover and inscribed "The Gift of Her Majesty 25th of Jan. 1842 To George Grinnell - O. Delawarr, Lord Chamberlain" (ref.1482).

Again no explanation as to why "W.T. Quinn" received his Bible "Given by The Bishop of Liverpool In Rememberance of Dec. 20, 1805. 1 Tim.4.14-16" - perhaps the reason might be interpreted from the biblical passages quoted (ref.0553).

Many simply stated "Thomas Nowell, the gift of my father, Christmas 1877" (ref.0377).

ENLISTMENTS AND RECORD OF SERVICE

The Cambridge pocket edition of the Holy Bible would have been much appreciated when it was "Presented to Arnold W. Round as a token of high esteem and goodwill from the members of the Young People's Service on the occasion of him joining His Majesty's Navy with the hope and prayer that he may find strength, council and guidance from its Sacred pages. Dated this 22nd day of July 1917. On behalf of the members. Signed: Leonard Smith, Joseph H. Round" (ref.1525).

A piece of paper inside a Family Bible noted, "The appointment of the Rev. Mr. Richard Langtry to be Chaplain of the Resolution - 11th day of February 1779" (ref.0128).

Noted in this family register was - "John Wakefield son of George and Margaret Wakefield of Uttoxeter, Staffordshire Born 3rd May 1826. Served 21 years in the Army chiefly in India discharged with the Rank of Sergeant and a permanent Pension of 1s.5.1/2d per day" (ref.0286).

"Private James William Grainger age 22 years Canadian Army Pay Corp. enlisted in Canada October 26th 1914, returned to England May 24th 1915 and went to the fighting line in the Great War, was married November 17th 1917 at Christ Church Enfield to Mary Victoria Lee age 20 years" (ref.0024).

A one line entry in the Bible is all that is written for "Timothy Jones born 1808 enlisted in the year 1826 discharged 1846" (ref.0090).

The Brown Family Bible records "September 28, 1901. T. Brown received Kruger Shilling from Archie Wood of the Rough Riding Imperial Yeomanry" (ref.0351).

"George Ashford enlisted for the Coldstream Regiment of Guards on the 14th November 1863? at Exeter - Regimental Number 692" (ref.0510).

"Charles Mills sailed for the Crimea 1855 October 16 in his 35 years" (ref.1413).

APPRENTICESHIPS AND INDENTURES

A Bible bought by John & Anne Gibben, on account of their daughter "Elizabeth who went to live (*sic*) servant with Mr. Greene(or Greave) at Backwell the 8th day of May 1754. And it pleased the Lord to take her out of this world the - day of October 1754. And it was thought proper to lay out the money she got in A Holy Bible which she took great delight in reading. She was 19 years of adge Agust ye 5, 1754. John & Anne Gibben. Their Book Bought in Chesterfield the 30th day of Octr.1754 price one pound". Many years later the owners of the same Bible wrote the following words "When our sister Elizabeth Ashton departed this Life on the 19th day of December 1840 She was the first of the Fameley that died - our ages all together when she died amounts to 648 Years, 4 Months, 1 Week, 2 Days" (ref.0314).

The words "Presented by the Wardens of the Goldsmith's Company to James Stocker on his being Apprenticed at Goldsmith's Hall. 3rd March 1880" were written inside the Bible (ref.0263).

On another occasion "This Bible was presented to John Mathews by the Reverend Thomas John Martin(?) on his leaving the Sunday School Gittisham. About the age of 12 years he went in the Service of a Clergyman where he lived 8 years, much respected he departed this life in the 26 year of his age at Taunton in the County of Sommerset in the midst of life we are in death" (ref.1227).

"My son Moses went to Mr. Hambleton of Chesterton Nov.11th 1824 and his indenture was made April 18th 1825, tailor". It would appear to be the Bible of Ralph Barlow and his son. "Moses Barlow was born November 1st at one o'clock in the morning in the year of our Lord 1812 Christened at Woolstanton November 22nd" - Moses was just 12 years old at the time of his Indenture (ref.0356).

"William Swinscoe put apprentice to Painter & Glazier Feb. 8, 1859 in his 15th year" (ref.0552).

"Edward J. Mackay started to serve his apprenticeship on the 20th December 1893 and was 18 years of age on the 22nd February 1894" (ref.0413).

"Robert Frayne b.23.10.1843 - 29.12.1856 bound to Mr. Hill till 21" (ref.1460).

"James Nichols was bound as apprentis[sic] to Mr.Ford April the 4th 1837" (ref.1481).

And almost a century before "Charles Francis bound apprentice to Mr. Robt. Aldersey clothier in the city of Chester Jan.y.13, 1752" (ref.0600).

Learning tools

EMIGRATION

There were many entries recorded in Family Bibles of whole families or sons or daughters who left home for some distant land probably never to be seen again. Here are some of those.

AMERICA/USA

According to the Family Bible, James Binns and his wife Alice Thistlewaite and their nine children left England in the year 1818 for Fayette County, Pennsylvania, USA (ref.1236).

"John Blake son of William & Maria Blake was born at Bradford June 5th,1817. Left England for America Nov.29,1842" (ref.0327).

There is no clue to the birthplace of the children of William & Sarah Jane Blunden, except for "Eliza Jane born 14th January 1824 near Pittsburg at America" (ref.1228).

"Richard Ellis & Abel Nicholas left Tywardreth (Cornwall) for America April 16,1840" these were the words written inside the Bible belonging to the Buzza family (ref.0242).

Another family who possibly saw their children sail away from Kent was recorded in the Family Bible "Richard Jarvis Harriot Buckman George Capeling Susannah Jarvis 4 children 3 boys and girl(sic) they left Bethersden for America Friday October 27/1848. Rec.d letter Ap 5/49" (ref.1084).

The Squires Family Bible simply states "John Squires born March 21st,1825, son of Samuel and Sarah Squires. Went to California 1854" (ref.0531).

This Family Bible notes the following persons who may have emigrated earlier "Sydney Newson born 30th June 1827 died in America April 3rd 1855; Robert Newson born 22nd Jan.ry 1823 died June 11th 1855 in America (both) buried at Cypress Hills Cemetery New York" (ref.0252).

It would be helpful to know exactly where this man died "Caleb (Simpkins) born 16 April 1834, died 30 Dec.1860 in America" (ref.0340).

The Lowen Bible simply records "Charles Mills sald for Amica February 16 1865 in his 44 years" and repeated the entry stating he "Sailed from England for America" (ref.1413).

Then there was "Elijah Alma Farrer (who) died at Pittsburg, USA on 26th August 1907" (ref.0211).

Just one entry in the Bible of the Snowden family mentions America - "Maud Eleanor (Snowden) dau. of Wm. Ch. Snowden born at Jersey City, New Jersey, USA 13/12/1913" (ref.0376).

"Stephen H. Searancke married 31st May 1922 to Lena dau. of Mr.& Mrs.Belloni, Grafton, California USA, married at Oakland, San Francisco" (ref.0386).

The Bible of David Cook contains the information that it was presented to him from his sisters Elizabeth Ann and Margaret Julia on his 25th birthday. November 3rd, 1895. Below this, appear the words "Mrs E.A. Knight sailed from Liverpool for Kearney, New Jersey, USA", [also] "Thomas Cook [aged 80 years] sailed from Liverpool to Kearney, New Jersey, USA. Dec.20/[19]24. s.s. Caronia C deck cabin 96 No.3 table, 36." (ref.0775). [NB: 1881 census for Farnworth, Lancs. shows a Thomas Cook age 37 with son David 10 and daughters Elizabeth 7 and Margaret 2. It would seem that the father Thomas Cook joined his children in the USA as a widower rather late in life, according to David's Bible inscription].

AUSTRALIA

Australia features quite predominantly in Bible inscriptions especially around the time of the goldrush! "My son David Tunbridge sailed from St.Katherines (Dock) London for Australia to the Gold Diggings June 15th 1852 on board the Holyrood, Capt. Stott Commander" (ref.0984).

The flyleaf in this Bible simply states "William Andrews born October 16th 1831. Left London for Hobart Town July 17th 1854 Married to Ellen Stannard May 9th 1861. Died May 3rd 1896 at Hobart" (ref.0854).

EMIGRATION 55

Mother saying goodbye

"H.George and M.A.Wall sailed from Gravesend in the ship Hydrabad on the 4th of September 1852 for Australia". The family obviously kept in touch because the entry is followed by "H.George died in Australia May 17th 1868 in his 81 year." Assuming it is one and the same H.George then he was 65 years old when he emigrated! In the same Bible "F.N. George and M.A. George with their children F. & A. George sailed from Gravesend in the ship New

Great Britain Oct. 29, 1854 for Australia". However the Bible does not explain the relationships to the other couple. (ref.0493).

"Fred died in his sleep at Melbourne Australia in a home for aged. Had lived in Melbourne many years heart failure" so said the Walker Family Bible, unfortunately with no date given (ref.0250).

The following information comes from a Family Bible bought in a junk shop in Semaphore, Port Adelaide, Australia and was a gift to "John Harris, Standlake, Oxfordshire from the Reverend Frank Burges, curate of his native village 1848". Entries relate to children of Thomas Harris who married Susannah Hanslow in 1812 of which there is an entry for a John Harris born 1815. So are they John's parents and siblings? (ref.1333).

"Charles John Hicks born November 14th 1864 Left for Australia April 3rd 1890 ship Wilcania. 2nd time November 1st 1895. Married to Lucy Beatrice Toutcher October 7th 1902" (ref.0854).

A simple entry "The boys David, John and Jem going to Australia September the 12,1911" (ref.0092).

No other information given in the inscription for "Anne Elizabeth Hirst, died 27th Dec.1928 aged 71 in Australia" (ref.0198).

Many descendants of the Lowen family appear to have emigrated............"Ellenor M. Mills sailed for Austrilia[sic] July 22 1852 in her 29 years of age" also "Mary Mills saild for Austrilia August 25 1854 in her 28 years" (ref.1413).

NEW ZEALAND

"My son William Tunbridge sailed from East India Dock, London on board the Roman Emperor for New Zealand on the 23rd November 1862." An earlier son David sailed to Australia, during the gold rush - see above entry. (ref.0984).

According to the Family Bible on, "15 Nov. 1859 Charles Ferrers Knyvett married Hannah Fanny Gregg in the parish church of Beddington, Surrey" - just only a year later is written "30th Dec.1860 Lilian Frances baptised in the parish church of Christ Church, New Zealand" (ref. 0994).

Sailing ships

On the flyleaf of a Holy Bible is written "New Zealand April 11th. To Mary Ann Edith Moss for her 13th birthday March 29th, 1902 From her Aunt Eleanor Moss With Kind Love & Best Wishes" [ref.0110].

"Christren Jane Mills sald for New Zeland July 13 1862 in her 73 years" on "Echunga" according to the Family Bible of the Lowen family (ref.1413).

Descendants of Londoner John Croucher (b.1811) and Mary Ann Cryer are all listed in the Croucher Family Bible as living in New Zealand and Australia to this day (ref.0023).

CANADA

Amongst the baptisms and marriages of the Family Bible the words "Henery York with his wife and five children left Long Buckley for Upper Canada, North America June 29th 1844" (ref.1186).

"Josiah Albert Burden married January 22nd, sailed February 24th,1920 to Toronto". Another entry states "Agnes Burden wife of Francis Burden, Canada died 9/4/44" (ref.0012).

"Samuel Body to Margaret Emily Bird at the Cathedral, Calgary, Alberta, Canada on the 29th April 1908" (ref.0451)...and in the same Bible is the following entry, "William Bird to Miss Ann Linklater October 5th 1910 by the Rev. Cannon Hinchcliffe at the home of John Hepburn, Sumas, Br. Columbia" (ref.0451).

"Cecil Groombridge married Freda Betty Bindall at Hamilton, Ontario, Canada Feb.12th 1944" (ref.0457).

CHANNEL ISLANDS

"William George (Walker) died Aug.9th 1895 at Jersey, Elizabeth (Walker) died Aug.28th 1897 at Jersey at 7.30pm William also died & was buried Jersey" (ref.0250).

The family of Angel/Duplain all seem to have been born in Alderney from 1847 (ref.0154).

"Archibald Augustus Atkins and Elizabeth Annie Lucy (married) 19.10.1903 Guernsey" (ref.0177).

INDIA

"August 29,1938 (married) to Capt. H.F. Richardson in Kasmir State, he died there March 10, 1943" entry from Newson/Grylls Family Bible, although who the captain married is not clear! (ref.0252).

"Thomas James Redan Farrer died at Ahenednugga, India on February 20th 1881. Soldier 7th Regt." (ref.0211).

ITALY

A rather unexpected place of birth for "John McDonald born Italy 1792 (and married to Catherine McLean) died Tarbert (Scotland) 20 Dec.1850". Many of their descendants lived in New Zealand some years later (ref.0348).

CANARY ISLANDS, SPAIN

An Atkins Family Bible entry reads "1902 Maud Alice home from Las Palmas (Canary Is.)" (ref.0177).

EGYPT

"Eileen Violet Chappin born Oct.29,1912 Cairo, EGYPT" (ref.0184).

WEST INDIES

Difficult to determine who wrote the following "John Anderson my brother died December aged 25 in the WEST INDIES AD.1817" (ref.0214).

SOUTH AFRICA

"Eleanor (Goodenough) born 15 Aug.1875 married Feb.5th,1898 G.A.Soltan-Symons Capt. King's Royal Rifles at St.George's Cathedral in Cape Town (South Africa)" (ref.0621).

A Bible printed in German and belonging to the McGibney family of Ireland, lists a great many family events, prizes and awards as well as "James E. McGibney sailed for South Africa, 25th April 1903", "James E. McGibney from S.Africa, arrived 16th July '06, sailed again to S.Africa, Hallow Eve '06", "James E. McGibney returned to Great Britain Jan.1918. Visited Donaghagny Aug.1918 after 16 years residence in S.A. Returned to Donaghhagny on Dec. 31st 1918" (ref.0692).

The Family Bible of the Lowen family lists many of the family emigrating including "Ellenor Mills sailed for the Cape of Good Hope the 29th of March 1848 on board of the Duke of Roxburgh in the 25 year of her age & 5 months" (ref.1413).

"Edith Dorothea (Osmond) Evans sailed for S. Africa on the ss Pretoria Castle from Southampton Nov.6th 1952 seen off by her sister Irene Mary Jenks, Maurice Jenks and her good friend Bill White" (ref.2276).

PHILIPPINES ISLANDS

"Edward Henry (Walker) died at Manila, Philippine Islands Aug.2nd 1898 and was buried there in the English Cemetery. He died during the war with USA and Spain after having served his country as British Consul for 38 years and was about to retire on a well merited pension" (ref.0250).

DEATHS AND THEIR CAUSES

Most Family Bibles record the dates of deaths and burials and occasionally the cause of death. Often a stillborn birth would be listed just like any other child in the family and sadly, even miscarriages have been recorded for posterity. "George Osbaldiston Harwood born the 4th day of Sept. 1874 son of the above of this city [Manchester] after this a misscarriage on the 24 May 1876." (ref 1393).

Sometimes you will find the odd comment - such as that written after the entry of the birth of "Thomas Randall born Sept. 1856 died same day. Doctor did not attend in time" (ref.0344).

Or the rather clinical annotation to an entry for... "Alice Mary (Hardman) died Thursday afternoon at 4.30 on Feb. 21st 1884, buried Feb. 25th at St. Stephens Church, Barbourne (enlarged spleen, bronchitis and other complaints)". One can't help wondering if it was the same Alice Mary baptised at home less than two years earlier (ref.0028).

Unfortunately this entry just says "Robert William Frayne born 29.9.1868 died 9.9.1888 during an operation in Grimsby Hospital" (ref.1460) similarly, "Gladys Christina Lankester died under operation" no date or cause given (ref.0987). Another Bible entry gives an amazing amount of detail "George Carrington married to Selina Ann Lampit Haines on 27 Aug. 1821 & went to live at Buckingham on the 3rd of June 1822 in the business of a butcher, but died of an inflammation in the bowels 1st January 1823, in the 24th year of his age. He had one child which died in a few days before him about 10 weeks old. They are both in one grave at Buckingham" (ref.0478).

The Family Bible of the James family tells of a now familiar cause of death.... "Jane Eliza Harding married to Cornelius James at Old Church Birmingham Aug. 2nd 1842, died with Cancer in the Breast June 3rd 1855 aged 41 years" (ref.0523).

Another sad entry was for "Archibald Watson Tinn 30 March 1883 Died at school 10 years" (ref.0445).

Many overseas deaths were fondly recorded by families at home such as "Edward Henry (Janion) died at Manila, Philippine Islands Aug. 2nd 1898 and was buried there in the English Cemetery" (ref.0250).

Or the sadly missed "Ernest Edward Gabriel died of disease in Mesopotamia. Beloved chauffeur "one of the family" aged 23 born March 17th ?1893?" (ref.2276).

An equally sad lament was for "Louise Randall born - about my own age - Eugene St, St.James Bristol married July 19,1849 St Martin in the Fields, Westminster Died Sunday Novr. 1, 1891. For over 42 years My Good Gentle and Faithfull wife, Buried in Reading Cemetery, the Memory of the Good survives and truly lives pleasant in our memory" (ref.0344).

It was a very sad day when "Prince Albert died December 14th 1861" - recorded in the Line Family Bible (ref.0036).

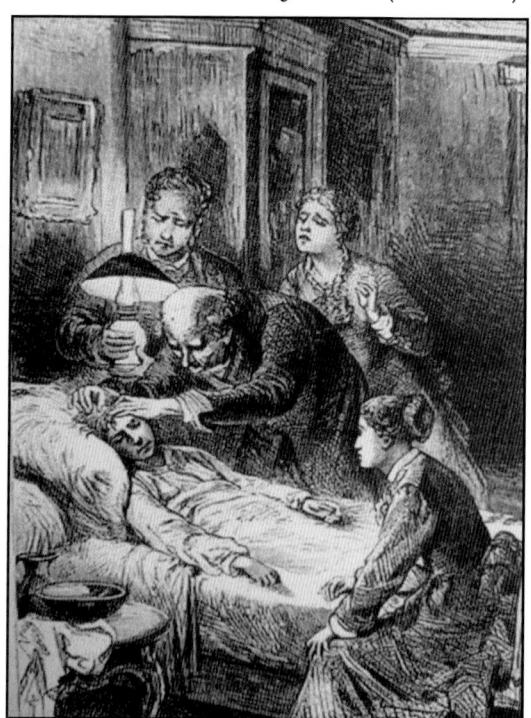

Doctor and patient

DEATH BY DROWNING

Written in the Swanton Bible "James Malcolm Pasley Swanton born on 23rd January 1887 and baptised at St. Paul's Church, Stonehouse, Devon - accidentally drowned at Indore, Central India 15th Feb.1907" (ref.0240).

Sadly "Francis Barnes 1st child Eldest son lost at sea on 12th June 1898. Washed overboard from s.s. Howick Hall (whilst on a voyage from Cardiff to Nagasaki, Japan) of which ship he was the 3rd Officer" so says the Barnes Family Bible (ref.0163).

According to a Jones/Ellis Family Bible, four men of the same family all died by drowning, perhaps they were fishermen? (ref.0037).

A certain James Dyson Bourne Baldrey is recorded as "Drowned 22 July 1909 buried at Lower Edmonton Cemetery, London" (ref.0053).

"Edwin Frayne b.1.9.1877 - lost at sea 29.6.1910" (ref.1460).

The Family Bible of John White reveals "John Charles White (born 1825) was drowned in Watford Harbour Nov.1838; Joseph Richard Hellyer White (born 1827) was drowned over Portland beach April 6,1845; William Barnard White was drowned September 27, 1872" (ref.0062).

A simple Bible entry reads "30th Aug. 1829 Death of James Charles, drowned at Burrs aged 67. Buried 2nd September" (ref.0500).

DEATH BY ACCIDENT

There are no doubts at all as to the cause of death of.... "My Aunt Matilda Robinson met with her death by an Omnibus on Monday April 4th 1853 was killed on the spot instantanesly aged 37 yrs" (ref.0309) or of the troubled "Sarah Jane Jones, [who] jumped in the Pit Oct.26th 1892" (ref.0043).

Just occasionally, a Family Bible will reveal a wealth of unique family history information such as the following inscriptions "My son John Sills Tunbridge died August 10th, 1860 at the Maypole Hotel, Nottingham having left his home at Handsworth Birmingham on 31st July, on the 3rd Augt. he was taken with Epyleptic and died after 7 days not being conscious from the time he was taken, he lays buried in the Handsworth Old Churchyard. Aged 41 years and 10 months" (ref.0985). Also written in the same Bible "Stephen Tunbridge departed this life July 4th 1869 at 6.45am age 74 years. His death resulted from an accident of falling down stairs and breaking his ribs in the morning of the 14th June. Doctor Massey attended him during his illness. An inquest was held on the body on July 8th (which we did not expect). He was buried on the same day at Forest Road Cemetery next to his eldest daughter Ann. He was followed to his resting place by his sons, Stephen Sills, Norley, Henry and Edward. Grave No.2929." Immediately following this and just a few weeks later, comes this sad entry, "Anne widow of Stephen Tunbridge was stricken with Paralysis on the 27th July 1869 and died at a quarter past seven in the morning of the 2nd August" (ref.0984).

A visit away from home ended rather sadly for "Thos.Veevers father to the above children, (who died) in Manchester on a visit to see his brother James. Died Thursday Aug.15th,1816 and interred in Todmorton churchyard Aug.17th Saturday" (ref.0450).

Insight into family sorrows are written in the following words "Eliza wife of Francis Bullock took to her bed on 31st Dec,1885 and died of a hemorrhage and exhaustion on 16th March 1886. During her illness she was assiduously attended by Mr.J.Bankart and she was buried on 20th March in the Exeter Cemetery close to her dear son Willie, the Revd. T.W. Cheynell officiating" (ref.0984).

Accidents on a much larger scale such as that of "James Games (second son and third child of John & Mary Games) had the misfortune of losing his father in the Prince of Wales Colliery Explosion Abercarn on September 10th 1878 and his mother was left a widow with five young children and a postumous child was born four months after her widowhood and she reared him (the latter) to 16 months" (ref.0120).

Other entries just state "Edward Charles Webster Killed in Pit. 18 Jan.1916 aged 33" (ref.0525).

A suspicious cause of death for this unfortunate lady? "At the R.A. Barracks, Clonmel, about 3 o'clock in the morning of Monday the 15th April 1878 Mary Dorothea Lloyd: age 40 on 23 March, died rather suddenly from extreme exhaustion, the result of excessive vomiting. Buried in the Churchyard of Parish Church,Clonmel". In the same Bible it was noted under the Deaths that, "At Johannesburg on June 7th,1915 Nellie Elizabeth Campbell died of diptheria caught nursing her son Arthur - buried at Johannesburg June 8th 1915" (ref.0313).

```
Great is the loss in early life
To seven children and a wife,
A tender husband and father dear
Who in him found a friend sincere,
His life was short and great his pain
We hope in heaven to meet again.
```

HARKNETT Bible (ref. 0958)

DEATHS BY SUICIDE AND MURDER

There is rather a sad tale written on a note pinned to the Family Bible of Carrington and Wickham. Perhaps it relates to a family relative or friend, "Mr. Pierce on that Recd the Taxes with Esq. Boydes Shot him Self in London the beginning of Jan. 1812 he wrote the words before he shot him self off Eclesiastes ye 9th Chap. & the 11th and 12th Verses. Look in the book and see. He went with Esq.
Boydes many years to Receive Taxes" (ref.0478).

One of the most memorable entries of all the inscriptions in the collection, is the following shocking incident written and spelt exactly as it appears in the Bible..... "Agust 19 1826 John Hall 92 yor and Richard Scot 85 your of age fought in the ospitle and John Hall kild Richard Scot with the blose that he got and Scot dide on the 21 of that month" (ref.0492) recorded presumably by the keeper of the Stainbank Family Bible in whose Bible it is written. Perhaps it happened in the 17th century Almshouses at Kirby Ravensworth, North Yorkshire known today as The Hospital?

WORLD WAR ONE DEATHS

Many Bibles recorded the untimely death of their loved ones whilst serving "in the great war" or "fighting for his country". The following are just a few selected entries.

"In loving memory of Pte. John Byatt 2341 Royal Fusiliars. Killed in action in France 20th April 1917. Gone but not forgotten. Sadly missed by his father & mother and sisters & brother & relations". He was just 21 years of age (ref.0239).

Even younger was "Albert Edward Syrett born March 26th 1897 Registered at Lambeth Killed in Action 3rd July 1915. Interred Boulogne, France" (ref.0426).

Many unfortunates are affectionately recorded in the Family Bible "Edward Frank Chubb born 6 August 1893 killed at Loose 26th September 1915, MISSING" (ref.0395).

"Laurence Harold Frayne b.18.9.1890-13.10.1915 reported wounded and missing" (ref.1460).

"George Frederick Tompkins born Dover Castle 14-3-1879 died Palestine, Killed in Action 13-11-1917" (ref.0129).

The Walker Family Bible simply records "William George Raw killed in action 2nd November 1917", although he is likely the same person who just four years before married Emily Rose Walker at Harlesden Parish Church (ref.0468).

A stark statement, "Abraham John Jones born Feb.24.1895 Died in the Great War Nov.8,1918" was all that was written (ref.0322).

"Captain James Frederick Sparrow aged 76 of 619 Third Ave. West, Buried in the field of honor Burnsland Cemetery Canada" (no date given) (ref.0135).

Rather shocking was the following inscription recorded in the Family Bible, "In British East Africa while on active service July 16th 1916, Capt. William Henry Aloysius Lloyd 122nd Nappatana Regt. attached 101st Grenadiers, was killed on the line of march by a sepoy striking him on the head with his rifle - aged 34 - buried in the cemetery near Sandeni, B.E.Africa" (ref.0313).

The entry in the Filer Family Bible simply reads "William Jordan Filer missing from Air Operations over Berlin Jan. 27, 1944" (ref.1502).

Soldiers on the move

WHERE THERE'S A WILL .....

Rather intriguing is the following statement written inside a Family Bible - but was it legal? "Feb.15,1921. This is to certify that everything that we posses & all things as furniture & every other thing that we have got we leave to our son George absolutely at our death & no one to interfeare for he as been a good son to us both. Signed Father Mr. A. Asbury Mother Mrs. Ann Asbury X Feb.15. 1921 - Mr & Mrs Asbury, 4/162 Brearly St, B.ham" (ref.0085).

Another declaration of a similar kind noted inside the Bible - the literal transcription "Witness my hand this day the 13th April 1869 (?) George Cox. George('s) name is put by the nurse by [h]is orders as he was not able to use [h]is arm [h]is self. BATH UNITED HOSPITAL. My Dear Wife Brother and Sisters All, I believe that I am about to part frome this life I sincerely hope to a far Better above all that I can do is to thank you all for your kindness and ask you all to See me put away as will my circumstancy Will alowe and to part my goods among you in fair way to defrey the expenses of my funerall I wish you all will and I sincerely hope and trust that the Lord will have mercy on my Soul and receive me into is Kingdom above" (ref.0205).

Or imagine knowing your ancestors very last words. Inside the front cover is recorded "Hannah Lancaster my wife died Sunday morning quarter past 8 o'clock Feby 14th 1847 in the 78th year of her age. Her last words were "Mercy is thy darling attribute, but judgement is thy strange work, have mercy upon me, shine into my soul"; and in one minute after departed as calm as a lamb". Hannah was the wife of John Lancaster (ref.0308).

In this burial inscription, the names of all the "paul" bearers are listed. "My dear wife Tabitha (Thompson nee Baldwin) departed this life July 2nd at half after 4'ock after a severe illness of nearly two years which she bore with Christian fortitude. Buried on Thursday afternoon at 5'ock in a brick vault at the south west end of the church, and the dear infant that died in 1828 before mentioned taken up and put in another coffin and set on top of its poor dear mother's coffin. Carried to church by: Chas. Short, - Machim, - Reed, Robt. Rowsore sen, Wm. Rowsore, - Denniss, Paul Bearers: Mr. Adams, Mr. Barker, Mr. Smith, Mr. Broks, Mr. Towers, Mr. Martin. If I die while at East Kirkby, [I] should like to have the same carriers and paul bearers if alive and child(?) to have top taken off and made large enough for two to lay broadside and for me to have an English Oak coffin, 1¼ins. thick and shell 1in. and ¾ Red Deal inside one. John Thompson, Agust 1832" (ref.1363).

The following was obviously of the utmost importance to the writer and needed to be recorded in a safe place, where better than in the Family Bible? "My Deeds left at my brother Williams at Latchford near Warrington November 23rd 1833 and I received Eighty Five Pounds on Mortgage Thomas Hancock witness Ralph Barlow" (ref.0356).

Finally a man of means! "Enoch Ffloyd Dyed a batchelor at his house in Chelsea in 1731 aged 74 and gave the bulk of his fortune to his nephew John Peck and his niece Elizabeth Peck and his great nephew George Peck Son of John Peck amounting to about £7,000 and appointed his Great Nephew George Peck his sole executor and was buryed near his Sister in Chelsea Church Yard in the County of Middlesex." So says the Family Bible of the Peck Family (ref.0963)

NOTABLE DAYS AND WEATHER

Special days and the weather were often noted when recording an important family event. In the Adams Family Bible, a birth was noted as "John Poynor son of Tho. Poynor was born 27th December 1691 being ST. JOHN'S DAY" (ref.0002).

"Agnes Burden wife of Francis Burden, Canada, died EASTER DAY 9/4/44" (ref.0012).

It was noted that... "Anne the wife of John Gibbons departed this life January 21, 1769 she was 54 years of age on OLD ST.MARKS DAY 1768" (ref.0314).

Then there was the weather "1893 Drought from March 2nd to May 21st, except single shower 15th April"....this was presumably written by Mary Bedingfield who was "presented by her Affectionate Father & Mother May 1870" a copy of the Holy Bible (ref.0025).

Was the weather ideal when......? "Harvest started in the midel of Jouley in the yore our Lord 1826 and aviney drought semer which had not been knowen for meney yores I sopose abought 50 yorback....." (*sic*), so wrote the owner of the Stainbank Family Bible (ref.0492).

Extremes of weather were obviously unusual events even in the old days when "A great storm of wind took place which took place on Friday October 14, 1881 blowing 200 trees down on Shardlows Estate Amersham Bucks" (ref.0036)... (It is interesting to note that the great hurricane which caused massive destruction in the 1980's in England also occurred about the same time in the month of October.)

It was so bitterly cold that it was worth recording in the Bible "memorandum of the time that the frost hold, began Dec.23.1739 ended Feb.10.1739/40", so says the Higson/Jones Family Bible (ref.0311).

72   THE FAMILY BIBLE: A PRICELESS HEIRLOOM

Often nothing more memorable than just..... "it was a very cold day"....being November 25, 1851 the day Louise Randall married Charles Shaw at St.John's Church in Reading.(ref.0344).

However, something very unusual happened on the night of "Sept.7th 1820 Edward (Thackray) our second son born, A Great Eclipse that Day" (ref.0104).

Bibles and Candle

SHORT VERSES AND POEMS

(Richard Blacled) A.D.1643.
He mee bote by right and enquiry;
If he it lose and you it find,
Restore it me againe
And bee so kind. (ref.1202)

Jonathan Jones his book AD.1732.
If I (?should) loose and you it find
I pray for you to be so kind
as to restor it me againe
and I will requit you for your paine (ref.0311)

Mary Stephenson Thy Godly Book.
A man of words & not deeds,
is like a garden full of weeds.
Remember Thy Creator (.....?.....)
Francis Cowles is my name 1650 (ref.0083)

Elizabeth Hicks is my name
England is my nation
Lower Sewell is my dwelling place
And Christ is my salvation. c1821 (ref.0055)

James Bending his book 1828.
Steal not this book for fear of shame
for above you is the owners name
the rose is red the grass is green
the days is past that I have seen (ref.1281)

The rose is red the leaves is green
The days is past wich I have seen
When I am Dead toll the bell
Take up this Book and use it well.
Jane Ann Bottomley. c1855 (ref.0725)

William Morgan 1705.   This Book
God gave him Grace herein to Look
Steal not this Book (for) fear of shame
because you see the owners name (ref.0601)

Thomas Fenemore his book (1879)
God give him grace there in to look
and not to look but understand
for learning is better than House and Land.   (ref.0200)
[and]
When House and Land is gone and spent
Then Learning is most Excellent. John Wynn (ref.0277)

William Giles 1722.
The Book my name shall ever have
When I am dead and in my grave
The greedy worms my flesh doth Eat
Ere you may read my name compleat. (ref.1077)

MISCELLANY

Wycliffe Bibles
In 1993, three early 15th century Wycliffe handwritten Bibles were bought at Sotherby's in London for £211,200.00 - the Bible's size about the same as a pocket dictionary. A few years ago valuations estimated the cost of a single Bible to exceed a staggering £1.3 million pounds.

Tyndale Bible
A complete copy of Tyndale's first edition Bible of 1526 was held by Bristol Baptist College until April 1994, when it was bought privately for one million pounds by the British Museum. The only other surviving copy, unfortunately incomplete, is held in St. Paul's Cathedral Library in London.

Erznka Bible
It was not many years after the publication of the King James Version of the Bible in 1604, that an illustrated Armenian Bible dating back to 1269 was discovered. This particular manuscript, normally housed in the Armenian Patriarchate in Jerusalem, went on display at the British Library in the year 2000. It was the first time in its history that the Erznka Bible had been loaned and it provided the centrepiece to an Armenian Christian Art exhibition being staged at that time.

The Good News Bible
Within ten years of its publication the unprecedented circulation record of sixty million copies worldwide was achieved, thus becoming Britain's top selling Bible right up to the present day.

British & Foreign Bible Society

In 2004 the British & Foreign Bible Society celebrated it's Bicentenary at St.Paul's Cathedral in London. The event was addressed by the Archbishop of Canterbury with over two thousand guests from Bible Societies from all over the world attending. Today the Scriptures have been translated into over 2000 languages worldwide.

Saint John's Bible

During 2006 The Victoria & Albert Museum in London displayed a "21st Century" Bible made in Wales, which was written by hand using paint made from gold, silver and lapis lazuli and was thought to have cost more than £2 million pounds. The Bible was commissioned by Saint John's University, Minnesota, USA and it was the first time it had gone outside the United States. Using medieval techniques, it still managed to contain illustrations referring to modern day situations.

King James Bible

The 400th Anniversary of the first edition of the King James Bible, started in 1604 and finally completed in 1611, was celebrated in the year 2011. No other Bible has influenced the English language to such an extent, mainly thanks to sailors and explorers who carried a copy of the Bible with them to all corners of the world. There are many common sayings attributed to the King James Bible such as – 'A sign of the times' – 'A law unto themselves' – 'Nothing new under the sun' – 'See eye to eye' - 'Sour grapes', to name just a few! Today fewer than two hundred original 1611 printings are known to exist and just occasionally one is unexpectedly found. Such was the recent discovery by parishioners in a Wiltshire church, of the Bible which "had always stood on a shelf at the church" and was found to be a rare 400 years old original King James Bible!

Theophilus Smith Bible

Relatively modern in comparison with the old family history Bibles, was the Bible of Mr. Theophilus Smith, farmer of Attleborough, Norfolk. Theophilus' inventive genius, by improving the common plough, caught the attention of the Earl of Albemarle who requested he bring his model to Windsor Castle in August 1841. There he was introduced to Prince Albert and also Queen Victoria, who showed great interest in his invention. Shortly after his return from Windsor, Theophilus received a magnificently bound quarto Oxford Bible with the following inscription on the fly-leaf: "Presented by command of Her Majesty to Mr.Theophilus Smith, Hill Farm, Attleborough, Norfolk. Oct.1st 1841". Sometime later he managed to obtain signatures of both Queen Victoria and Prince Albert to complement the Bible's authenticity. Sadly Mr. Smith died in 1848 and the family heirloom was then passed to his eldest son. He was also named Theophilus, and through his friendship with the Royal party on visits to Sandringham, he successfully managed to obtain the autographs of thirteen other Royal personages for the Bible. Alexandra, Princess of Wales; Albert Edward, Prince of Wales; Christian, Prince of Denmark; Louise, Princess of Denmark and Princess of Hesse; Frederick, Prince of Denmark; Dagmar, Princess of Denmark; George, Duke of Cambridge; Frederick William, Crown Prince of Prussia; Victoria, Crown Princess of Prussia; Alice, Princess of Hesse; Louis, Prince of Hesse; Alfred, Duke of Edinburgh; Arthur, Duke of Connaught.

On the death of Mr.Smith's eldest son, the Bible descended to a daughter Mrs Page who settled in South Africa. [Printed in the Methodist Recorder dated 1906.] (ref.2245).

Lunar Bible

It may come as a surprise to learn that Bibles have already landed on the moon! A great many organisations and individuals were involved in helping achieve this historical fact. It was on February 5, 1971, Apollo 14 Lunar Module Pilot Edgar D. Mitchell succeeded in landing the first Bible on the moon when lunar module Antares touched down on the moon's surface. Earlier Bibles had been carried on Apollo 12 and 13, but none had successfully landed on the surface of the moon. Due to weight restrictions it was deemed necessary to find a Bible small and light enough to be carried on board. This was achieved by microfilm technology which enabled a small piece of film, the size of a colour slide, to include 1245 pages and 773,746 words of the Bible. Multiple copies of the microfilm were carried on Apollo 14 and these became known as the Lunar-Landed Bibles.
Website: http://ApostlesofApollo.com/first-lunar-Bible

The NET Bible

Another modern day phenomenon launched in 2005 was the NET Bible and as the name suggests it is in fact an internet Bible, the initials standing for New English Translation. It began in 1996, took nine years to produce and is being continually updated online. With over 60,000 footnotes, it looks set to be the definitive modern translation of the Bible.
Website: www.Bible.org/netBible

Bible Dicing!

An amusing story, relating to Bibles, appeared in a Huntingdonshire newspaper some years ago with regard to a recent ceremony dating back to 1678, where as many as twenty-four children from churches around St. Ives in Cambridgeshire, gathered together to listen to a sermon given by Father John Pullen. This was followed by a centuries old ceremony called Bible Dicing, where they rolled two dice, throwing for the highest score, before being awarded a new Bible. According to Father Pullen, this event has taken place every year since, as confirmed by the number of elderly folk in town who received Bibles as young children. The ceremony appears to be unique for the town of St. Ives and it was said to have originated from a bequest in the Will of Dr. Robert Wild, who died in 1675 leaving £50 to the parish church to provide six Bibles to six local children. His Will states "every year twelve children, six males and six females, shall cast dice for six Bibles". Dr.Wild, a Non-Conformist and with an obvious mischievous sense of humour, requested that the dice be rolled on the Communion table, but as a compromising gesture for today's modern ceremonies, a special table is set up beside the altar.

The Internet

Finally, a true story about a Family Bible lost and then found, thanks to the power of the internet. Around 1970, a man was searching for a spare part for his car in a scrap yard on Merseyside when he came across some books in the boot of a car about to be crushed. Seeing that one of them was a tattered leather bound Bible, he opened it to discover that it contained vital family records for the surnames of Sherwood and Morgan dating back to 1820 in villages around Ashford and Wye in Kent, but no addresses to give a clue to the last owner. He kept the Bible, hoping that one day he might find the family who owned it. Then early in 2005 he passed it on to his daughter in Norwich who had just got access to the Internet. She did a search on Google for the surnames and places mentioned which produced a unique match with the Sherwood family tree on the personal website of Phil Sherwood. She then sent an email to Phil entitled "Great News of Biblical Proportions" and it was soon established that the Bible had originally belonged to his three times great-grandmother Elizabeth Sherwood (ref.2256).

SOURCES

Throughout the writing of this book, I have been very fortunate in being able to consult many published and unpublished archives, official records, newspaper and magazine reports as well as the original Bible inscriptions themselves sent by many people over the years. My thanks to all. Special thanks to Tracy St. Claire for the inscriptions she allowed me to incorporate into my collection and to staff at all the record offices and libraries who were most helpful at all times.

A History of the Geneva Bible, Vol. One
Act of Parliament 1783 - Tax of Baptisms
Apostles of Apollo website: http://ApostlesofApollo.com/first-lunar-bible
Bible Society Bicentenary Issue March 2004
Bible Society Journals & website: www.biblesociety.org.uk
Biblical Studies Foundation website: http://bible.org/netbible
Bucks Free Press, Maidenhead & Marlow Journal 1938
"The Daily Telegraph" 29/1/2006
"The Evening Standard" 26/4/1994
"The Guardian" 27/4/1994
Hertfordshire Archives and Local Studies
Huntingdonshire Newpaper Archives
"The Independent" 28/5/1994
Lambeth Palace Library Catalogue
Lord Wharton's Trust & Charity
"Methodist Recorder" 1906
Miscellanea Genealogica et Heraldica
History of England and Great Britain 1899, Prof. Meiklejohn
A Bible for Wales 1988, Prys Morgan
"The Sunday Express" 18/12/1994
The British & Foreign Bible Society
Illustrations: ReusableArt.com
OldBookIllustration.com
FromOldBooks.org
WPClipart.com

SURNAME INDEX

Adams 31, 70, 71
Aldersey 52
Allandson 27, 29
Allen 41
Anderton 47
Andrews 54
Angel 58
Arnold 41
Ashford 48, 50
Ashton 51
Atkins 58, 59

Baldrey 63
Baldwin 38, 69
Bambridge 27
Bankart 65
Barker 29, 30, 45, 70
Barlow 51
Barlow 70
Barnes 63
Bebb 44
Bedingfield 46, 70
Belloni 54
Bending 73
Beverley 32, 33
Bill 30
Bindall 58
Binns 27, 53
Bird 58
Blacled 72
Blake 52
Bloss 32
Blunden 53
Body 58
Bohun 39
Bonwicke 38
Bottomley 74
Bowyer 22
Boxall 44
Boydes 66

Broks 70
Browings 44
Brown 24, 35, 44, 50
Buckman 53
Bullock 64
Burden 58, 70
Burges 56
Burns 5, 25,
Buston 44
Butler 40, 41
Buzza 53
Byatt 67

Campbell 65
Cantuary 45
Capeling 53
Carrington 61, 66
Cartmell 27, 30
Carver 47
Challoner 16
Chappell 25, 26
Chappin 59
Charles 20, 25, 63
Cheynell 65
Chubb 67
Coalman 45
Collamore 36
Cook 54
Corles 45
Cousens 44
Cove 30
Coverdale 17
Cowles 73
Cox 69
Croucher 47, 51
Cryer 57

Dandridge 34
David 30
Davidson 46

Davies 25, 30
Davis 44
Delawarr 49
Denman 38
Denniss 70
Dibben 41
Dolton 44
Drover 41
Duplain 58

Ellis 53, 63
Evans 49, 60

Fairman 31
Farrer 54, 58
Fenemore 74
Ferguson 23
Ffloyd 32
Filer 68
Fitzgerald 5
Forbes 45
Ford 52
Foskett 41
Fowle 28
Fownes 36
Fox 24, 43
Francis 29, 52
Frayne 52, 61, 63, 67
Fullilove 27, 29

Gabriel 62
Games 65
Gay 44, 48
Geldart 48
George 55
Gibben 38, 51
Gibbons 71
Giles 74
Good 35
Goodenough 45, 59
Goodwin 11
Grainger 50
Gram 46
Greave 51
Green 43, 51
Gregg 56
Griffin 43

Grinnell 49
Groombridge 58
Grove 42
Grylls 58

Hadfield 45
Haines 61
Hall 48, 66
Hambleton 51
Hancock 70
Hanslow 56
Harding 29, 61
Hardman 61
Hardy 45
Harris 56
Harvey 27
Harwood 34, 35, 61
Hatherley 38
Hatson 38
Haughton 23
Heard 23
Hemert 48
Hicks 56, 73
Higson 30, 70
Hill 52
Hinchcliffe 58
Hiron 35
Hirst 12, 56
Holtham 25
Howarth 45
Hull 12
Hunt 27, 30
Hurst 40
Hutton 41

Impey 12
Isaacs 26

James 61
Janion 62
Jarvis 53
Jenks 60
Jenner 34
Johnson 38
Jones 20, 30, 38, 50, 63, 64, 67
  71, 73

SURNAME INDEX

Kaull 45,
Keiller 5,
Kennedy 5,
Kensington 35,
Kerr 45,
Kerstemeem 48,
Kingwell 37,
Kinsky 45,
Knight 48, 54,
Knyvett 56,

Lamb 5,
Lancaster 69,
Langtry 50,
Lankaster 61,
Latham 25,
Lee 50,
Levinson 39,
Line 62,
Linklater 58,
Llewellyn 44,
Lloyd 65, 67,
Lowen 54, 56, 57, 60,
Lucy 58,
Luther 38,

Machim 70,
Mackay 52,
Madox 28,
Martin 41, 51, 70,
Massey 64,
Mathews 48, 51,
Matthew 17,
Matthews 41,
Maxwell 25,
McAdam 5,
McArthur 47,
McDonald 59,
McGibney 59,
McLean 59,
McRobbie 13,
Mercer 12,
Milding 47,
Millard 43,
Mills 50, 54, 56, 57, 60,
Morgan 19, 74, 79,
Morris 24,

Mortimer 47
Moss 57

Nash 37
Newport 44
Newson 53, 58
Newton 41, 48
Neyland 41
Nicholas 53
Nichols 52
Nickols 30
Noble 44
Norton 30
Nowell 49

Osmond 26, 60

Page 77
Paine 23
Parker 45
Parsons 41
Pearson 25
Peck 32
Pierce 66
Poynor 28, 71
Pullen 78

Quarrington 44
Quinn 49

Randall 61, 62, 72
Raw 67
Reed 70
Richardson 58
Rigden 27
Robinson 43, 48, 64
Round 50
Rowsore 70

Sampson 48
Sanders 45
Scot 66
Searancke 54
Seddon 48
Shaw 72
Sherwood 79
Short 70

Simpkins 54
Simpson 32
Skinner 41
Sleidan 38, 39
Small 38
Smith 43, 45, 50, 70, 77
Snowden 54
Soltan 59
Soper 45
Sparrow 67
Spragg 45
Squires 53
Stainbank 66, 70
Stanley 41
Stannard 54
Stephenson 73
Stewart 42
Stocker 51
Stonestrete 27, 31
Stott 54
Suffolk 43
Swanton 63
Swingler 40
Swinscoe 51
Symons 59
Syrett 67

Thackray 72
Thistlewaite 53
Thomas 30
Thompson 69, 70
Tinn 62
Tompkins 67
Toutcher 56
Towers 70
Tunbridge 54, 56, 64
Tyndale 17

Veasey 43
Veevers 64

Wakefield 50
Walker 54, 56, 58, 60, 67
Wall 55
Wanstall 41
Warren 28
Watson 40
Way 47
Webster 65
Wesson 46
West 43
Westbury 40
Wharton 10, 11, 12, 13, 40
Wheler 34
White 33
White 49, 60, 63
Whitting 45
Whittingham 19
Wickham 66
Wild 79
Williams 35, 40
Willing 44
Wilson 36, 40
Wollaston 25
Wollstein 25, 42
Wood 32, 50
Woodmass 25
Worthington 38
Wycliffe 13, 16
Wynn 32, 74

Yate 42
York 58

PLACE INDEX

Abercarn 65
Adelaide 33, 56
Ahenednugga 58
Alberta 58
Alderney 58
America 21, 53, 54
Amersham 71
Antwerp 17
Ashford 79
Attleborough 77
Australia 33, 47, 54, 55, 56
Austria 45
Ayr 25

Backwell 51
Bala 20
Barbourne 61
Bath 34, 69
Beddington 56
Bedingfield 46
Berkley 45
Berlin 68
Bethersden 53
Birmingham 61, 64, 69
Blackfriars 35
Bletchley 45
Boulogne 67
Bradford 53
Bristol 17, 28, 62, 75
British Columbia 58
British East Africa 67
Buckingham 61
Buckinghamshire 10, 71
Burnsland 67
Burrs 63

Caernarvonshire 19
Cairo 59
Calcutta 34
Calgary 58

California 53, 54
Cambridge 77
Cambridgeshire 78
Canada 50, 58, 67, 71
Canary Islands 59
Canterbury 19, 75,
Cape of Good Hope 60
Cape Town 59
Cardiff 63
Carnsore Point 23
Channel Islands 58
Chelsea 70
Chester 52
Chesterfield 38, 51
Chesterton 51
Chilham 45
Christchurch 56
Claines 44
Clonmel 65
Clough Heigh 27
Connaught 77
Cornwall 53
Crimea 50
Cumberlandshire 10

Deal 41
Denmark 77
Devon 63
Donaghagny 59
Dover 67
Dublin 23
Dundee 5

East Ham 41
East Kirkby 70
Edinburgh 77
Edmonton 63
Egypt 59
Elstree 37
Enfield 50

85

86 THE FAMILY BIBLE: A PRICELESS HEIRLOOM

England 34
Exeter 37, 48, 50, 65

Farncombe 33
Farnworth 54
Fayette County 53
France 26, 67

Geneva 18
Germany 16, 17, 38
Gittisham 41, 51
Gloucestershire 45
Grafton 54
Gravesend 55
Grimsby 61
Guernsey 58

Hamilton 58
Handsworth 64
Harbrough 40
Harlesden 67
Harpenden 25
Harrogate 47
Hawkhurst 37
Helpston 46
Henley Upon Thames 34
Hesse 77
High Wycombe 11
Hobart 54
Huntingdonshire 78

India 50, 58, 63
Indore 63
Irchester 41
Ireland 23, 59
Italy 59

Japan 63
Jersey 58
Jersey City 54
Jerusalem 75
Johannesburg 65
Jordan 26

Kashmir 58
Kearney 54
Kent 37, 53, 79

Kinsale 28
Kirby Ravensworth 66
Kirkby Bain 40

Lambeth 45, 67
Lancashire 54
La ngham 45
Las Palmas 59
Latchford 70
Leeds 41
Leningrad 11
Liverpool 49, 54
LLanfairfechan 25
Llanfihangel-y-Pennant 20
London 6, 17, 20, 29, 30, 32, 38, 47, 54, 56, 57, 63, 66, 75
Long Buckley 58
Lower Sewell 73

Manchester 34, 44, 48, 61, 64
Manila 60, 62
Melbourne 47, 56
Merioneth 20
Merseyside 79
Mesopotamia 62
Milton 40
Minnesota 75

Nagasaki 63
New Barnet 44
New Jersey 54
New York 53
New Zealand 47, 56, 57, 59
Norfolk 77
North Finchley 44
North Leith 41
North Yorkshire 66
Northswitch 38
Norton 41
Norwich 79
Nottingham 64

Oakland 54
Ontario 58
Ordsall Hill 48
Oxford 11
Oxfordshire 56

Palestine 67
Pembroke 44
Penhurst 23
Pennant 20
Pennsylvania 53
Petham 27
Phillippines 60
Pittsburg 53, 54
Portland 63
Prussia 77

Reading 42, 62, 72,
Richmond 13

Salop 42
San Francisco 54
Sandeni 68
Sandringham 77
Scotland 25, 59,
Shorwell 47
Sinningthwaite 10
Somerset 51
South Africa 59, 60, 77
Southampton 60
Southwark 49
Spain 60
St.Ives 78, 79
St.Kilda 48
Staffordshire 50
Standlake 56
Stonehouse 63
Suffolk 45
Sumas 58
Surrey 32, 56
Swan Hill 40
Swinshead 40

Tarbert 59
Taunton 51
Thornwill 47
Tipperah 34
Todmorton 64
Toronto 58
Twyford 44
Ty Mawr Wybrnant 19

Upton Magna 42
USA 53, 60
Uttoxeter 50

Vienna 45
Vilvorde 17

Walcot 34
Wales 19, 20, 24, 75, 77
Wandsworth 32
Warrington 70
Watford 63
Wellington 42
Wells 45
West Indies 59
Westminster 62
Westmorland 10
Wexford 23
Wheathampstead 25
Wiltshire 75
Windsor 77
Woburn 43
Wolstanton 51
Wooburn 12
Worcestershire 44
Worms 17
Wycombe 10
Wye 79

Yorkshire 10

Vessels
Caronia 54
Ceres 23
Duke of Roxburgh 60
Echunga 57
Holyrood 54
Howick Hall 63
Hyderabad 55
Melville Castle 34
New Great Britain 55
Pretoria Castle 60
Resolution 50
Roman Emporor 56
Wilcania 56